Confident & Free

Grow in Godly Confidence Through Intimacy with God

Erin Lamb

Confident and Free
Published by Lamb Enterprises LLC
Dublin, Ohio 43016

ISBN: 0692123180
ISBN-13: 978-0692123188

DEDICATION

Freedom is never voluntarily given by the oppressor;
it must be demanded by the oppressed.
Martin Luther King, Jr.

To all who have felt shackled by insecurity, fears, and low self-worth, this is for you! You are an overcomer! You are more valuable than the rarest diamonds. You were created to be the best version of yourself! You were created to live confident and free.

CONTENTS

INTRODUCTION 1

DAY 1: GOD SAID CREATION WAS VERY GOOD 3

THE GOSPEL: JOINING THE FAMILY OF GOD 7

DAY 2: REDEEMED BY THE SACRIFICE OF JESUS 9

DAY 3: TRANSFORMED BY LOVE 13

DAY 4: CUSTOM MADE BY GOD 17

DAY 5: CREATED WITH DIVINE PURPOSE 21

DAY 6: CONFIDENT IN GOD'S PROVISION 25

DAY 7: PROTECTION FROM OUR ENEMIES 29

DAY 8: CONFIDENCE IN THE STORM 33

DAY 9: CONFIDENCE IN PERSECUTION 37

DAY 10: CONFIDENCE WHEN FACING DEATH 41

DAY 11: GIVEN AUTHORITY IN JESUS NAME 45

DAY 12: STRENGTH IN INTIMACY WITH GOD 49

DAY 13: DISCERNMENT AND TESTING ALL THINGS 53

DAY 14: CONFIDENT IN THE PROMISES OF GOD 57

DAY 15: GIFTED AND INCLUDED 61

DAY 16: FULL ACCESS GRANTED 65

DAY 17: EMPOWERED TO LAVISH GIVING 69

DAY 18: CONFIDENCE WHEN FACING REJECTION 73

DAY 19: HEALED AND WHOLE IN THE SOUL 77

DAY 20: CONFIDENT IN FRIENDSHIP WITH GOD 81

DAY 21: CONFIDENT IN CRISIS   85

DAY 22: CONFIDENT WITHOUT PERFECTION   91

DAY 23: FREEDOM FROM SHAME   95

DAY 24: ACCESS TO THE CONTENTMENT OF GOD   99

DAY 25: FREEDOM FROM TRAUMA   103

DAY 26: FREEDOM FROM THE OPINIONS OF MAN   107
(PEOPLE PLEASING)

DAY 27: FREEDOM TO UNDERSTAND SPIRITUAL   111
THINGS

DAY 28: FREEDOM TO REST   115

DAY 29: FREEDOM TO CREATE   119

DAY 30: FREEDOM TO DREAM   123

BONUS POEM: DO YOU KNOW WHO YOU ARE?   127

CONCLUSION   133

ABOUT THE AUTHOR   135

INTRODUCTION

We live in a culture that can create issues in the esteem of every person. Every place you turn, there is a new supplement, a new diet, a new procedure, a new something to make a person more appealing, beautiful or handsome, or accessible.

The beauty industry works overtime to discover the primary insecurities of humans, then they work to capitalize on those insecurities.

Much of marketing is geared towards convincing humanity, "Who you are is simply not enough. You need to change who you are to be someone more appealing, more youthful, or more of something. What you have is not enough. You need to buy more, earn more, be more."

There is nothing wrong with wanting to be desirable, beautiful or handsome, or appealing. The issues arise when there is substantial dissatisfaction with who God created, and the thirst for more becomes an addiction.

Vanity is a trap. Lust for more is a trap. Overindulgence of self is a trap.

The devotionals included deposit God's word into the soul and spirit with the hopes godly confidence emerges. What am I trying to sell you, nothing? I desire to draw you deeper into the heart of God.

The next 30 days are about intimacy with God and growing to know who we are in relationship to God. One cannot understand the real value of something without knowing the Creator, and its creation purpose.

Let's begin with prayer. Know I am praying for you throughout this journey of godly confidence and freedom.

Papa God, I ask for every person who reads this devotional to have profound encounters with you. I pray for walls to come down and restoration of hearts. Have your way, Lord. I ask that every seed of your word sown falls on fertile ground. Water it with your Spirit. Remove any lies believed and replace them with your truth. Deliverance is first a truth encounter. I ask for godly confidence to arise. Reshape and remold identities into the image created by your Son. We are your artistry created for your glory. Let your beauty saturate our spirits and souls. In Jesus mighty name.

DAY 1:

GOD SAID CREATION WAS VERY GOOD

• • • *G*od said, "Let Us make man in Our image, according to Our likeness; let them have dominion over the fish of the sea, over the birds of the air, and over the cattle, over all the earth and over every creeping thing that creeps on the earth."

So God created man in His own image; in the image of God He created him; male and female He created them. Then God blessed them, and God said to them, "Be fruitful and multiply; fill the earth and subdue it; have dominion over the fish of the sea, over the birds of the air, and over every living thing that moves on the earth."

And God said, "See, I have given you every herb that yields seed which is on the face of all the earth, and every tree whose fruit yields seed; to you, it shall be for food. Also, to every beast of the earth, to every bird of the air, and to everything that creeps on the earth, in which there is life, I have given every green herb for food;" and it was so. Then God saw everything that He had made, and indeed it was very good. So, the evening and the morning were the sixth day (Genesis 1:26-31 NKJV).

DEVOTION

God has good ideas, and you (we) were one of them. When God looked at creation pre the fall of humanity, He stated it was very good. Very is an adverb or adjective that can mean, "to a high degree, exceedingly," according to Webster's dictionary.

There was no part of God's heart that was not in love with creation. God set the universe in place; the first beings made in God's image were on the earth. To be created in the image of God does not mean God looks like us. It says we have a mind, will, emotions, intelligence, consciousness, the ability to create, to feel, to laugh, to reason, to speak, to exercise a will (choose), and God gave male and female the ability to procreate (produce children after their kind).

Humans are the only beings stated in scripture made in God's image. We are the only ones capable of redemption. Angelic beings and demons do not have the same privileges afforded to humankind.

REFLECTION

How does it make you feel to know you were God's idea?

Does it change your perspective to realize God thought creation was exceptional?

PRAYER/DECLARATION

Papa God, help me to see myself the way you do. I was created in your image and designed to be an object of your incredible love. You have great thoughts about me. You created me for a reason and purpose. You looked upon creation and said it was very good. Help me to see as you see with the eyes of love.

GOD SAID CREATION WAS VERY GOOD

I decree and declare God created me in His image according to Genesis 1. My intended heavenly lineage is royalty. I was destined to be a part of God's family. I am fearfully and wonderfully made (Psalm 139).

THE GOSPEL:
JOINING THE FAMILY OF GOD

Before we go any further into devotions, I would like to give you an invitation to know Jesus and be a part of God's family. Unfortunately, if you continue to read Genesis, you will see that Adam and Eve chose to obey the devil instead of God. Their decision cost them and each of us substantially. Sin entered the picture and tainted the identity of humanity.

The good news is Jesus, the Son of God, came to redeem the world for the choices of Adam. What does this mean for us? Since the penalty for sin is death, we can through repentance and faith in the Son be made right with God. We can accept by faith His sacrifice for our sins and appropriate His righteousness. He paid a debt we could not pay.

Contrary to popular belief, everyone is not God's child. Adoption into the family of God comes through receiving the Son. Jesus plainly stated that no one came to the Father except through Him (See John 14:6).

Would you like to be a part of God's family? I will tell you that this involves a giving of one's entire life to God. It is not merely a prayer we pray with plans to live independent from God. It is similar to accepting a marriage proposal. We are inviting God into our lives to have all of it, not just parts of it. He moves into our hearts, and the transformation occurs from the inside out. Change is not about trying to clean yourself up all by yourself. The first step is admitting we have sinned against a holy God and the second step believing in the Son by faith.

I am here praying as I type that you accept the invitation to know Jesus as Savior and Lord. He paid the highest price out of selfless love. It has been the best decision I have ever made.

Will you pray with me?

God, I admit I have sinned against you and your precepts. I acknowledge that I am in desperate need of a savior. I ask for your forgiveness for all of my sins. Cleanse my heart and wash it clean. I pray for Jesus to be my Savior and also to be Lord over every area of my life. I believe He is your Son, born of a virgin, crucified, and raised on the third day. He is entirely your Son and fully God. Jesus, I invite you into my heart, my spirit, my life and to be Lord. I place my faith in you. I choose from this day forward to follow you. Make me completely new. I want, as an act of my will, to devote my life to you.

If you sincerely said this prayer, I would love to hear from you! Welcome to the family of God.

I highly encourage getting into a healthy community of followers of Jesus, baptism as a symbol of your new life in Christ, and reading the bible. If you do not own one, check out biblegateway.com, or blueletterbible.com. I recommend starting with the New Testament in the book of John.

DAY 2:

REDEEMED BY
THE SACRIFICE OF JESUS

*B*lessed be the God and Father of our Lord Jesus Christ, who has blessed us
with every spiritual blessing in the heavenly places in Christ, just as He chose
us in Him before the foundation of the world, that we should be holy and
without blame before Him in love, having predestined us to adoption as sons by Jesus
Christ to Himself, according to the good pleasure of His will, to the praise of the glory
of His grace, by which He made us accepted in the Beloved.

In Him we have redemption through His blood, the forgiveness of sins, according
to the riches of His grace which He made to abound toward us in all wisdom and
prudence, having made known to us the mystery of His will, according to His good
pleasure which He purposed in Himself, that in the dispensation of the fullness of the
times, He might gather together in one all things in Christ, both which are in heaven
and which are on earth—in Him. In Him also we have obtained an inheritance, being
predestined according to the purpose of Him who works all things according to the counsel
of His will, that we who first trusted in Christ should be to the praise of His glory.

In Him you also trusted, after you heard the word of truth, the gospel of your salvation; in whom also, having believed, you were sealed with the Holy Spirit of promise, who is the guarantee of our inheritance until the redemption of the purchased possession, to the praise of His glory (Ephesians 1:3-14 NKJV).

DEVOTION

One of the noblest characteristics of God is His desire to redeem the lost. We all have sinned and fallen short of His glory, except Jesus (See Romans 3:23). Therefore, we are all in need of grace, mercy, and forgiveness. God is compassionate and gracious, slow to anger, and abounding in love (see Psalm 103:8).

God's great love for humanity meant He created a backup plan before we ever messed up to save us. Before God created the world, God knew us all. Before the world was created, God had a plan to save the world and to provide an inheritance for the world.

God is an incredible parent who longs to see His goodness imparted to His children.

We can be confident not only in God's love, we can be satisfied with God's provision. God provided the sacrifice for us, paying a debt we could never repay. When sin cried out, "Someone must die." God cried out, "I will take their place."

There is no greater love in the entire world. Love was poured out on the rugged cross to proclaim loudly, "You are of infinite worth!"

Being redeemed means the shackles of sin and shame can fall off. Shackles of sin were crushed under the power of God's love.

The value of something is determined by how much someone is willing to pay for it. Jesus gave his life. His sacrifice signifies the worth of every human being.

REFLECTION

Does knowing Jesus thought enough of humanity to give His life transform perceptions of your worth and the worth of others?

We can be confident of God's love based on the demonstration of Jesus' love on the cross. Does this change your view of your worthiness?

PRAYER/DECLARATION

God, I thank you for every spiritual blessing in the heavenly places in Jesus. I thank you for the invitation to be a part of your family and to know you. Thank you for the sacrifice of your Son. My freedom cost you significantly, and I thank you. Help me to see what it means to be an heir and child of God. Transform my thoughts, so I understand myself the way you do. You proved I was worth dying for, help me to live out this truth.

I decree and declare that since I have surrendered my life to Jesus, repented of my sins, that I am redeemed by His sacrifice. The old me has passed away, and the new has come. My new identity is a child of God. My inheritance in Jesus is rich, full, and can never be depleted. I am worthy of love. I am sincerely and profoundly loved.

DAY 3:

TRANSFORMED BY LOVE

Beloved, let us [unselfishly] love and seek the best for one another, for love is from God; and everyone who loves [others] is born of God and knows God [through personal experience].

The one who does not love has not become acquainted with God [does not and never did know Him], for God is love. [He is the originator of love, and it is an enduring attribute of His nature.] By this, the love of God was displayed in us, in that God has sent His [One and] only begotten Son [the One who is truly unique, the only One of His kind] into the world so that we might live through Him.

In this is love, not that we loved God, but that He loved us and sent His Son to be the propitiation [that is, the atoning sacrifice, and the satisfying offering] for our sins [fulfilling God's requirement for justice against sin and placating His wrath].

Beloved, if God so loved us [in this incredible way], we also ought to love one another. No one has seen God at any time. But if we love one another [with unselfish concern], God abides in us, and His love [the love that is His essence abides in us and] *is completed and perfected in us. By this we know [with confident assurance] that we abide in Him and He in us because He has given to us His [Holy] Spirit. We [who were with Him in person] have seen and testify [as eye-witnesses] that the Father has sent the Son to be the Savior of the world (1 John 4:7-14 AMP).*

DEVOTION

The love that God has for humanity is perfect.

Love does not initiate with us. Love comes from God to us and then through us. We have the job of receiving; we receive the perfect love of God which does not fail.

I love 1 John 4:8. It says the one who does not love does not know God because God is love. When we know God's love for us, it empowers us to appreciate and accept ourselves in healthy ways.

Healthy love is encouraging, inspiring, empowering, life-giving, forgiving, full of grace, and wisdom. The Father demonstrated His great love in sending His Son, and Jesus gave His life.

God expressed His love before we were worthy. God loved us before He forgave us. God loved us before we knew Him. The love God demonstrated is beyond what humans could express.

God's love pushes out pride, fear, insecurity, and low self-esteem. Perfect love says, "You are cherished, not based on how you look, perform, or behave."

Many of the issues with confidence are rooted in a lack of receiving God's love. The most significant thing about God's love is that it is not dependent on us. It is independent of our merit. Unlike human love which depends significantly on our behavior, performance, or appeal, God's love is pure and on full blast for us. Once we receive God's love, we are empowered to love others with the same passion God gives us.

REFLECTION

Do you feel loved by God? If so, why? If not, why not?

How does the revelation that God's love is not based on merit, behavior, or our love impact you?

PRAYER/DECLARATION

Father God, thank you for your love. It is a love that is unlike another. Thank you for a love that does not fail. I receive your love in its fullness. Please remove everything in my heart that is blocking me from receiving your love. I want to know the height, depth, width, and depth of your incredible love. It's so much more luxurious than anything I could ever encounter with a human being or understand.

I decree and declare that the love of God is more powerful than anything in the world. God's love is on full blast 24/7 for me. I am loved every moment of every day. I receive God's love and accept that I am 100% cherished. I am deeply loved. I choose to believe and receive God's love for me.

DAY 4:

CUSTOM MADE BY GOD

F or You formed my inward parts;
You covered me in my mother's womb.
I will praise You, for I am fearfully and wonderfully made;
Marvelous are Your works,
And that my soul knows very well.
My frame was not hidden from You,
When I was made in secret,
And skillfully wrought in the lowest parts of the earth.
Your eyes saw my substance, being yet unformed.
And in Your book they all were written,
The days fashioned for me,
When as yet there were none of them.
How precious also are Your thoughts to me, O God!
How great is the sum of them!
If I should count them, they would be more in number than the sand;
When I awake, I am still with You (Psalm 139:13-18 NKJV).

DEVOTION

Have you ever watched an artist paint or sculpt? Have you looked into the eyes of one who creates? Have you seen the excitement on the face of the one who with each brush stroke or move of their hands makes something beautiful?

You and I are God's incredible workmanship created for His glory. You are the canvas on which God chose to paint His astonishing creation. You are the clay God formed in His hands to make a vessel created for great glory. Most artists have a great fondness for their masterpiece. They value the work of their hands. To insult the artwork is to insult the artist. God is the artist. We are the artistry, and created by the hands of LOVE!

David, who wrote Psalm 139, stated that God's thoughts towards him were more numerous than the sands. God's thoughts are quite extensive.

"If you assume a grain of sand has an average size, and you calculate how many grains are in a teaspoon and then multiply by all the beaches and deserts in the world, the Earth has roughly (and we're speaking very roughly here) 7.5 x 10^18 grains of sand, or seven quintillion, five hundred quadrillion grains,"-www.npr.org.

God's thoughts are excellent and numerous towards us. God has great ideas about you. Let that sink in for a moment. I have probably had maybe 100 kind thoughts about my artwork, yet God has quadrillions of ponderings.

You and I are far more precious to God than a painting or sculpture: those things do not contain the breath of God. You and I are God-breathed creations who were custom made by God. There is no one on earth with the fingerprints of God on them identical to us. Even identical twins have some differences.

Custom things are highly valued, and sometimes far more valuable than mass produced things. You were thought of, shaped, and molded

18

by the hands of the greatest Artist of all time, God. Just look at the stars and the wonder of creation. God thought the world needed someone like you to walk the earth and display His handiwork.

REFLECTION

David penned such glorious words about God's love for him. God has a unique and profound affection for you too. List 5 things David states about himself in the passage provided.

1.

2.

3.

4.

5.

Now take those five things and insert your name in "I am," statements. Example: I am fearfully and wonderfully made.

1.

2.

3.

4.

5.

PRAYER/DECLARATION

Papa God, thank you for creating me beautiful/handsome. Thank you for your handiwork and the incredible thoughts you have about me. I accept your truth that I am fearfully and wonderfully made. God created me with His hands of love. I am cherished in the Beloved. My body, soul, and spirit were all created by you. I choose to accept your love, I recognize and agree with your thoughts about who I am and my worth. I am appealing by your standards which are the highest standards. I choose to value myself because you deem me highly valuable.

I decree and declare that I am beautiful/handsome. I reflect the handiwork of God. My appearance is no mistake. My DNA was custom made and handcrafted by God. I bless my body and soul. I am God's artwork. He delights in me and all the works of His hands.

DAY 5:

CREATED WITH DIVINE PURPOSE

A *nd you He made alive, who were dead in trespasses and sins, in which you once walked according to the course of this world, according to the prince of the power of the air, the spirit who now works in the sons of disobedience, among whom also we all once conducted ourselves in the lusts of our flesh, fulfilling the desires of the flesh and of the mind, and were by nature children of wrath, just as the others.*

But God, who is rich in mercy, because of His great love with which He loved us, even when we were dead in trespasses, made us alive together with Christ (by grace you have been saved), and raised us up together, and made us sit together in the heavenly places in Christ Jesus, that in the ages to come He might show the exceeding riches of His grace in His kindness toward us in Christ Jesus. For by grace you have been saved through faith, and that not of yourselves; it is the gift of God, not of works, lest anyone should boast. For we are His workmanship, created in Christ Jesus for good works, which God prepared beforehand that we should walk in them (Ephesians 2: 1-10 NKJV).

DEVOTION

We were created for good works before we ever knew God. Over the course of my life, I have heard people say they have no purpose or no sense of purpose. The questions pop up, "Why am I here? Why was I born? What is my life all about?" To know the use of someone or something, we must first possess some comprehension of the one who created the thing or person.

We learned on Day 1 that creation was God's idea. We learned on Day 4 that we were custom made by God. Today, we are exploring God's purposes.

We can learn from this passage and additional scripture that we are handcrafted to:

Be alive in Christ (Ephesians 2:1)

Receive the grace and kindness of God (Ephesians 2:7)

Receive the gift of salvation (for those who receive Him) (Ephesians 2:8)

Sit in heavenly places with Jesus (Ephesians 2: 6)

Do good works (Ephesians 2:10)

Know God (be in a relationship with Him) and abide in Him (John 15:4-5)

Enjoy God (Psalm 16:11)

Be recipients of God's love (John 3:16, 1 John 4:19, Psalm 103:8)

Be adopted into God's family (Ephesians 1:5)

Have abundant life (John 10:10)

Make Him known and make disciples (Matthew 28:19)

Care for the poor, widows, and orphans (James 1:27)

Bring God glory and bear good fruit (Revelation 4:11, 1 Corinthians 10:31)

This list is not exhaustive. There are many things incorporated in the Bible concerning God's purposes for us. The primary goal is a relationship with God. Everything else flows out of a relationship with God. Out of intimacy with God (knowing God) we find out who we are and our life's meaning.

My living out this list may look drastically different from yours, and that is perfectly okay. God is the Creator, not a cloner. Therefore, each child has a unique expression of His glory on earth.

REFLECTION

You and I are created for an intimate relationship with God. Do you find yourself doing more things for God than spending time with God? How can knowing God help define and fine-tune purpose?

Review the list of things we were created for, what stands out most to you and why?

List three passions. Do any of those things tie into a purpose on the list? How can you pursue those things for God's glory?

1.

2.

3.

PRAYER/DECLARATION

Papa God, thank you for creating me to do good works. I am not loved or saved based on my good works. My acts of kindness flow out of a relationship with you and out of receiving your great love. Please, purify my passions and help me to dream even more magnificent dreams with you. Help me to know you on a higher, deeper, and more intimate level.

I decree and declare that I am handcrafted by God for a divine purpose. I am a custom design that displays God's goodness and creativity on earth. My life has a purpose and incredible meaning. There are gifts and talents placed by God inside of me to bless the world. I am chosen to bring God fame. My purpose is deeply rooted in God.

DAY 6:

CONFIDENT IN GOD'S PROVISION

A nd the Lord spoke to Moses, saying, "I have heard the complaints of the children of Israel. Speak to them, saying, 'At twilight, you shall eat meat, and in the morning you shall be filled with bread. And you shall know that I am the Lord your God.'"

So it was that quails came up at evening and covered the camp, and in the morning the dew lay all around the camp. And when the layer of dew lifted, there, on the surface of the wilderness, was a small round substance, as fine as frost on the ground. So when the children of Israel saw it, they said to one another, "What is it?" For they did not know what it was.

And Moses said to them, "This is the bread which the Lord has given you to eat. This is the thing which the Lord has commanded: 'Let every man gather it according to each one's need, one omer for each person, according to the number of persons; let every man take for those who are in his tent.'"-Exodus 16:11-16 (NKJV).

25

DEVOTION

We read in Exodus 16 of the complaints of the Israelites. They had been held in captivity for hundreds of years. Moses was a deliverer for God's people. They went from slavery to freedom. They went from bondage to having the freedom to make choices. Instead of trusting the Lord who brought them out of Egypt for their every need, they focused on what they did not have. How many times do we forget what God has done, and not recall who He is? How many times does our short memory lead to unbelief? God has revealed so much in His word about who He is and His incredible intentions for us. How easy it is to forget the heart of God and the truth of His nature.

Even though the Israelites complained and grumbled against God, He provided. God provided quail and bread (manna). They still complained and disobeyed God.

It is in our human nature to focus on the bad instead of the good. It is human nature to complain and forget the goodness of God. It is in our best interests to remember. It is in our best interests to focus on who God is. It is in our best interests to focus on the nature of God.

God is called Jehovah Jireh-the Lord who provides. The provider is what Jehovah-Jireh means; the Lord Who will see to it every need is taken care of for His children. God knows our needs because He understands everything. God can meet our deficits at just the right time as He did for Abraham, and God can meet every necessity fully,-paraphrased from Bible.org.

God is exceptional at providing. Do we trust God? Part of confidence flows from knowing who God is and how much God loves us. If our faith is solely in ourselves, others, the economy, or our abilities, we will be uncertain and insecure. Our greatest confidence needs to flow from who God is and our relationship with God.

REFLECTION

List off some things God has done in the past for you. List ways God has miraculously provided. Write out an "I Remember List."

What thing(s) has been your focus? Take a piece of paper, write "God Will Provide" at the top. Place your concern(s) on that list.

PRAYER/DECLARATION

Papa God, I ask for your forgiveness for unbelief, murmuring and complaining. I thank you for all you are and all you have done. I want to be one who walks by faith and not by sight. Your name is Provider. I can trust you to meet all of my needs according to your riches in glory. I can place my full confidence in you.

I decree and declare that my needs are of utmost importance to God. What matters to me touches God's heart. God promises to meet all of my needs according to His riches in glory. God withholds nothing exceptional from me and is faithful to meet all my needs (emotional, physical, soul, and spiritual). My confidence grows as I place my complete trust in God.

DAY 7:

PROTECTION FROM OUR ENEMIES

Then David said to Saul, "Let no man's heart fail because of him; your servant will go and fight with this Philistine."

And Saul said to David, "You are not able to go against this Philistine to fight with him; for you are a youth, and he a man of war from his youth."

But David said to Saul, "Your servant used to keep his father's sheep, and when a lion or a bear came and took a lamb out of the flock, I went out after it and struck it, and delivered the lamb from its mouth; and when it arose against me, I caught it by its beard, and struck and killed it. Your servant has killed both lion and bear; and this uncircumcised Philistine will be like one of them, seeing he has defied the armies of the living God." Moreover, David said, "The Lord, who delivered me from the paw of the lion and from the paw of the bear, He will deliver me from the hand of this Philistine."

And Saul said to David, "Go, and the Lord be with you!"

So Saul clothed David with his armor, and he put a bronze helmet on his head; he also clothed him with a coat of mail. David fastened his sword to his armor and tried to walk, for he had not tested them. And David said to Saul, "I cannot walk with these, for I have not tested them." So David took them off.

Then he took his staff in his hand; and he chose for himself five smooth stones from the brook, and put them in a shepherd's bag, in a pouch which he had, and his sling was in his hand. And he drew near to the Philistine. So the Philistine came and began drawing near to David, and the man who bore the shield went before him. And when the Philistine looked about and saw David, he disdained him; for he was only a youth, ruddy and good-looking. So the Philistine said to David, "Am I a dog, that you come to me with sticks?" And the Philistine cursed David by his gods. And the Philistine said to David, "Come to me, and I will give your flesh to the birds of the air and the beasts of the field!"

Then David said to the Philistine, "You come to me with a sword, with a spear, and with a javelin. But I come to you in the name of the Lord of hosts, the God of the armies of Israel, whom you have defied. This day, the Lord will deliver you into my hand, and I will strike you and take your head from you. And this day I will give the carcasses of the camp of the Philistines to the birds of the air and the wild beasts of the earth, that all the earth may know that there is a God in Israel. Then all this assembly shall know that the Lord does not save with sword and spear; for the battle is the Lord's, and He will give you into our hands."

So it was when the Philistine arose and came and drew near to meet David, that David hurried and ran toward the army to meet the Philistine. Then David put his hand in his bag and took out a stone, and he slung it and struck the Philistine in his forehead so that the stone sank into his forehead, and he fell on his face to the earth. So David prevailed over the Philistine with a sling and a stone, and struck the Philistine and killed him. But there was no sword in the hand of David. Therefore, David ran and stood over the Philistine, took his sword and drew it out of its sheath and killed him, and cut off his head with it.

And when the Philistines saw that their champion was dead, they fled. Now the men of Israel and Judah arose and shouted, and pursued the Philistines as far as the entrance of the valley and to the gates of Ekron. And the wounded of the Philistines fell along the road to Shaaraim, even as far as Gath and Ekron. Then the children of Israel returned from chasing the Philistines, and they plundered their tents. And David took the head of the Philistine and brought it to Jerusalem, but he put his armor in his tent.

When Saul saw David going out against the Philistine, he said to Abner, the commander of the army, "Abner, whose son is this youth?"

And Abner said, "As your soul lives, O king, I do not know."

So the king said, "Inquire whose son this young man is."

Then, as David returned from the slaughter of the Philistine, Abner took him and brought him before Saul with the head of the Philistine in his hand. And Saul said to him, "Whose son are you, young man?"

So David answered, "I am the son of your servant Jesse the Bethlehemite." (1 Samuel 17: 32-58 NKJV).

DEVOTION

Goliath taunted David. Goliath, as noted in Scripture, was wearing 126 pounds of armor. He was bigger, stronger, and confident. Goliath's confidence was in his abilities. The abilities of our enemies are no match for God. David did not come in his strength. He came in the name of the Lord. He came in confidence based on who God was and who God had been for him in the past. David had an intimate relationship with the Lord.

Scripture tells us that those who place their faith in the Lord will not be shaken (Psalm 125:1). It does not mean there will not be adversity. Adversity will come. The point is where is our confidence, is our faith in ourselves or God? God is bigger and more magnificent than any giant we may face. God has infinite wisdom, insight, and strategies for overcoming.

Our strength lies in our intimacy and union with God. David had experiences with God that fueled his faith and confidence. We too can gain greater confidence through encounters with God. Learning to trust God is a process. We can grow in confidence by learning to trust God in the small things and then reflecting on those things when greater challenges come.

We can also grow in confidence by listening to the testimonies and victories of others. The word of God can build our faith and be a mighty tool in our hands. The story of David is not merely a history lesson; it is a tool in our hands when facing our Goliaths.

REFLECTION

Name one victory you have had with God. How did the experience of success/overcoming with God impact your confidence?

What can you take away from David's story that builds your confidence?

PRAYER/DECLARATION

Papa God, thank you for your unfailing love and building our confidence through our relationship with you. No matter the size of the giant, you are more prominent. We can trust in you to meet not only our needs, but we can also believe you as our protector. I place my full confidence in you. Remind me of the victories and help me to keep them in my remembrance.

I decree and declare that God is my protector. I can place my full confidence in God's abilities. It is not by my might or power; it is by God's Spirit. I am empowered by God's Spirit to be an overcomer like David. I am confident in God's goodness, love, protection, and provision. God is my defense.

DAY 8:

CONFIDENCE IN THE STORM

O n that [same] day, when evening had come, He said to them, "Let us go over to the other side [of the Sea of Galilee]." So leaving the crowd, they took Him with them, just as He was, in the boat. And other boats were with Him. And a fierce windstorm began to blow, and waves were breaking over the boat, so that it was already being swamped. But Jesus was in the stern, asleep [with His head] on the [sailor's leather] cushion. And they woke Him and said to Him, "Teacher, do You not care that we are about to die?" And He got up and [sternly] rebuked the wind and said to the sea, "Hush, be still (muzzled)!" And the wind died down [as if it had grown weary] and there was [at once] a great calm [a perfect peacefulness]. Jesus said to them, "Why are you afraid? Do you still have no faith and confidence [in Me]?" They were filled with great fear, and said to each other, "Who then is this, that even the wind and the sea obey Him?" (Mark 4:35-41 AMP).

DEVOTION

Jesus is the One the wind and the waves must obey. He was able to sleep through storms because He knew who He was and the goodness of the Father. Jesus lived out His identity with confidence. He was not arrogant, nor self-debasing. Jesus walked in peace, love, joy, wisdom, courage, authority, and humility. He did what He saw the Father doing (John 5:19).

There is such untapped and unused authority in the lives of some believers. Jesus was aware of the power He carried as the Son of God. We, in Christ, are invited into the family of God as children and heirs as well. Jesus told the disciples, "Behold, I give unto you power to tread on serpents and scorpions, and over all the power of the enemy: and nothing shall by any means hurt you," (Luke 10:19 KJV).

Jesus maintained peace, and therefore He could release order into the storm. Jesus was not timid in His approach to the storm. He sternly spoke to the storm to be still, be quiet. The wind and the waves had to obey His authority. The disciples marveled at His power. He said, "Why are you afraid, do you still have no confidence in Me?"

Confidence in God gives us peace in storms. Even when the winds and waves rage against us, we can stay in a place of peace, trusting that God is higher than the storm. Once again, our confidence is not in our ability. Our faith is in God's abilities. He is our peace and peace in every challenging circumstance.

REFLECTION

The disciples were afraid during the storm. When you are worried or scared, who is your contact person? How does turning to someone else help in challenges or in storms?

Jesus sternly rebuked the turbulence, taking authority over the storm. How do you address the storms of life?

What can we learn about the authority of Jesus over storms?

PRAYER/DECLARATION

Papa God, thank you for the authority given in your Son's name. At the name of Jesus, every knee must bow, every sickness bow, and everything not of you must bow. I ask for a deeper understanding of your authority and the authority I have in your name. I am not without help or a source of strength. I call on your name and rely on your power. You are all powerful and more powerful than the storms.

I decree and declare that in Christ I have been given power over the power of the enemy. I am not defeated. I am an overcomer. Nothing that comes to me is more powerful than who is in me. I can trust in the authority of Jesus over every obstacle and storm. God's name is more powerful than anything and everything. God's name is higher than any other name. I stand and overcome with the authority of Jesus.

DAY 9:

CONFIDENCE IN
PERSECUTION

The crowd also joined in the attack against them (Paul and Silas), and the chief magistrates tore their robes off them and ordered that Paul and Silas be beaten with rods. After striking them many times [with the rods], they threw them into prison, commanding the jailer to guard them securely. He, having received such a [strict] command, threw them into the inner prison (dungeon) and fastened their feet in the stocks [in an agonizing position].

But about midnight when Paul and Silas were praying and singing hymns of praise to God, and the prisoners were listening to them; suddenly there was a great earthquake, so [powerful] that the very foundations of the prison were shaken and at once all the doors were opened and everyone's chains were unfastened. When the jailer, shaken out of sleep, saw the prison doors open, he drew his sword and was about to kill himself, thinking that the prisoners had escaped. But Paul shouted, saying, "Do not hurt yourself, we are all here! "Then the jailer called for torches and rushed in, and trembling with fear he fell down before Paul and Silas, and *after he brought them out [of the inner prison], he said, "Sirs, what must I do to be saved?" (Acts 16: 22-30 AMP).*

DEVOTION

The church has endured persecution since its inception. Every person who wished to do the will of God has experienced some form of oppression. There is something about the Light of God that is offensive to the kingdom of darkness. If you walked into a room filled with rats and turned on the lights, they would scurry. Light hurts those who live in the dark. Our eyes are not accustomed to light if we have been living in the darkness.

In Acts 16, we read about Paul and Silas and their persecution for delivering a girl with a spirit of divination. Her deliverance caused a profit loss to her slave owners. They were falsely accused and brought before the magistrates. The claims against them were:

"These men, who are Jews, are throwing our city into confusion and causing trouble. They are publicly teaching customs which are unlawful for us, as Romans, to accept or observe," (Acts 16:20b-21). They were attacked and thrown in jail.

Believers are called to be salt and light in the earth. Salt preserves and light exposes and gives life. If the light shrinks back because of the darkness, the darkness increases. Someone must be willing to live in the light, host the light, and shine the light of God's goodness, love, peace, truth, and power in a world of deception.

The story of Paul and Silas does not end in persecution. It ends with the jailer coming to know Jesus along with those in his household. God works exceedingly well in challenging situations.

Scripture lets us know that persecution reveals where our confidence lies. Daniel suffered greatly under a wicked king. He did not bow to the evil or idolatry of his day. God rewarded Daniel significantly by not only protecting him from the lions in the lion's den, God placed his story on display for all the world to know that even if the world cast you into the lion's den, He is the deliverer. Paul and Silas focused on God and worshipped. God delivered His people, and other people were saved.

We can have confidence in our faithful defense system. Our unshakable defense and defender is God. The same God who delivered His people from Egyptian slavery stands in power for those who love Him and those called according to His name.

REFLECTION

What is your first response to persecution? Is your priority to focus on the Lord or the persecution?

How can we see a victory by focusing on the Lord?

What are two lessons you can take away from the story of Paul and Silas?

PRAYER/DECLARATION

Papa God, thank you for your saving and protecting power. Thank you that you are always with me and for me. I thank you that no matter how fierce or challenging the persecution, you will work all things together for incredible good. I trust you with every aspect of my life. I can remain confident in you in every season of life.

I decree and declare that no weapon formed against me shall prevail. When the enemy comes in like a flood, you promised to lift up a standard against him. You are working what the enemy means for evil for incredible good. When I submit to you, resist the devil, he will flee from me. I can be confident in all aspects of life.

DAY 10:

CONFIDENCE WHEN FACING DEATH

I *assure you and most solemnly say to you, if anyone keeps My word [by living in accordance with My message] he will indeed never, ever see and experience death." The Jews said to Him, "Now we know that You have a demon [and are under its power]. Abraham died, and also the prophets; yet You say, 'If anyone keeps My word, he will never, ever taste of death.' (John 8:51-52 AMP).*

Martha replied, "I know that he will rise [from the dead] in the resurrection on the last day." Jesus said to her, "I am the Resurrection and the Life. Whoever believes in (adheres to, trusts in, relies on) Me [as Savior] will live even if he dies; and everyone who lives and believes in Me [as Savior] will never die. Do you believe this?" (John 11:24-26 AMP).

DEVOTION

Jesus provided great hope and assurance for those who placed their faith in Him and followed Him. He said, "You will not die, but have everlasting life." He goes on to tell us in John 14:3, "... *I go and prepare a place for you, I will come back again, and I will take you to Myself so that where I am you may also be.*" This life on earth is temporary. Heaven is eternal. True believers will not taste the horrors of the afterlife apart from God. Followers of Jesus have a promise of something so much better in Jesus and with Jesus.

The promises of God are yes and amen in Christ. The temporary does not trump the eternal. Any believer facing death can be confident of their eternal destination, if they have been in union with Christ and following Jesus.

It is imperative that we remain in faith until we see God face to face. I mean saving faith. Scripture tells us, "Many false prophets will appear and mislead many. Because lawlessness is increased, the love of most people will grow cold. But the one who endures and bears up [under suffering] to the end will be saved. This good news of the kingdom [the gospel] will be preached throughout the whole world as a testimony to all the nations, and then the end [of the age] will come," (Matthew 24:11-14 AMP).

There is a promise of heavenly paradise for those who endure to the end. It is a promise worth looking forward to and holding dear. Those in Christ will not suffer eternal torment with the evil one. Therefore, believers can stand confidently when facing death. It is not the end of the story. Many believers were persecuted to the point of death; an earthly death was not their final destination. It is not ours either.

REFLECTION

Why can we be confident when facing death?

What does it mean to you to endure until the end?

What are some of the things we can look forward to in heaven? (See Revelation 21:4, Isaiah 25:8).

PRAYER/DECLARATION

Papa God, I thank you for defeating our worst enemy, death. I thank you for the sacrifice of your Son which paid for my freedom. I am eternally thankful for salvation and redemption. Thank you for blessing me beyond what I deserve. Help me to live confident in what I have received from you by faith. I have nothing to fear.

I decree and declare that death is not the final authority over me. The ultimate authority is God alone. I am no longer a prisoner of sin and death. I am not a prisoner of fear. You have not given me a spirit of fear, but a spirit of love, power, and a sound mind. If I abide in your love, I am free from fear and loaded with godly confidence. I declare that my life belongs to Jesus.

DAY 11:

GIVEN AUTHORITY IN JESUS NAME

He said to them, "I watched Satan fall from heaven like [a flash of] lightning. Listen carefully: I have given you authority [that you now possess] to tread on serpents and scorpions, and [the ability to exercise authority] over all the power of the enemy (Satan); and nothing will [in any way] harm you. Nevertheless, do not rejoice at this, that the spirits are subject to you, but rejoice that your names are recorded in heaven." (Luke 10:18-20 AMP).

"So, everyone who hears these words of Mine and acts on them, will be like a wise man [a far-sighted, practical, and sensible man] who built his house on the rock. And the rain fell, and the floods and torrents came, and the winds blew and slammed against that house; yet it did not fall, because it had been founded on the rock. And everyone who hears these words of Mine and does not do them, will be like a foolish (stupid) man who built his house on the sand. And the rain fell, and the floods and torrents came, and the winds blew and slammed against that house; and it fell—and great and complete was its fall."

When Jesus had finished [speaking] these words [on the mountain], the crowds were astonished and overwhelmed at His teaching; for He was teaching them as one who had authority [to teach entirely of His own volition], and not as their scribes [who relied on others to confirm their authority]. (Matthew 7:24-29 AMP).

DEVOTION

Jesus knew who He was. There was no insecurity in Him. He did not live in the realm of fear, doubt, uncertainty, unbelief, worry. Jesus spoke with authority. He spoke what pierced the hearts of those around Him. There was no pretense or desire to impress the crowds. He lived under the already given acceptance of the Father.

The authority the Father entrusted to the Son was given to born again, Spirit-filled believers. He gave the disciples power and authority over sickness, demonic spirits, and as stated by Jesus in Luke 10:19, all the power of the enemy.

Believers are not supposed to be tossed to and fro by a defeated devil. Believers are to live in a place of victory. God already won and gave believers the ability to operate in His authority.

Authority is not given to enforce our will on earth or people. God allows people to choose. Control is a fruit of witchcraft. Authority is given to align things with God's will, to protect, to empower, to elevate, and destroy the works of the devil.

Jesus did not just pay for salvation on the cross; He paid for freedom, deliverance, and healing. He gave believers the authority in His name to see the sick healed, the demonized set free, and many forces of darkness limited. Jesus already paid for it.

Once we know God and know who we are in Jesus, we begin to flow in God's confidence. It is not our authority; it is operating in the authority of Jesus. We can be confident that we are who God says we are and can do all He says we can do. When exposed to sickness, oppression, and works of the devil, we can pray in His authority for a breakthrough.

REFLECTION

What does it mean to walk in God-given authority?

What encouragement did Jesus give to help us maintain humility? (See Luke 10:18-20 passage).

What is the proper use of the power? (see Acts 1:8).

PRAYER/DECLARATION

Papa God, I thank you for the authority given in the name of your Son. Thank you, Jesus has the name above all names. Thank you for His wisdom and truth. I thank you for supplying all our needs including the spirit of an overcomer. Help me to walk in your authority, knowledge and insight, love, and with humility. Help me to use authority for heaven and your will on earth. Reinforce within me godly confidence.

I decree and declare that there is no name higher than the name of Jesus. God is the supreme authority and the only One to worship. I stand in His authority and not mine. I can be confident in who Jesus is and who I am in Him. I received power when the Holy Spirit came upon me. I am not powerless or a victim. I am empowered by God to do the works of Jesus.

DAY 12:

STRENGTH IN INTIMACY WITH GOD

M y sheep hear my voice, and I know them, and they follow me: *And I give unto them eternal life; and they shall never perish, neither shall any man pluck them out of my hand. (John 10:27-28 KJV)*.

DEVOTION

The voice of God is available to every believer. Straight from the words of Jesus, we are given the ability to hear from God. Part of intimacy is communication. Woven through the pages of scripture is God's interaction with humanity. He spoke to Moses through a burning bush (Exodus 3:1-17), Saul on the way to Damascus (Acts 9), God spoke to prophets of the old and new testament. God is relational. God speaks to His children (John 10:27).

God speaks through a still small voice, dreams, visions, impressions, circumstances, and in many ways to reach the heart of humanity. We encounter His voice in the pages of scripture, and God will not violate His word when communicating with humanity. He does expand our understanding. We may have learned something about God that does not adequately represent the heart of God. An example would be slavery in the United States was justified by many with scripture. It violated so many precepts of God (loving your neighbor as you love yourself, love does not harm its neighbor, love is the highest commandment).

We are not only invited to know the voice and heart of God, but Jesus also invites us to be one with Him. Part of being one is relationship and intimacy. We read in John 17:22-26 AMP the following words of Jesus:

I have given to them the glory and honor which You have given Me, that they may be one, just as We are one; I in them and You in Me, that they may be perfected and completed into one, so that the world may know [without any doubt] that You sent Me, and [that You] have loved them, just as You have loved Me.

Father, I desire that they also, whom You have given to Me [as Your gift to Me], may be with Me where I am, so that they may see My glory which You have given Me because You loved Me before the foundation of the world.

"O just and righteous Father, although the world has not known You and has never acknowledged You [and the revelation of Your mercy], yet I have always known You; and these [believers] know [without any doubt] that You sent Me; and I have made Your name known to them, and will continue to make it known, so that the love with which You have loved Me may be in them [overwhelming their heart], and I [may be] in them."

One implies closeness. It means proximity. It invites us to do life together. It implies a relationship. Our strength does not lie in our independence from God; it lies in our intimacy and dependency on God. Jesus stated in John 15:4-15 AMP, "Remain in Me, and I [will remain] in you. Just as no branch can bear fruit by itself without remaining in the vine, neither can you [bear fruit, producing evidence of your faith] unless you remain in Me. I am the Vine; you are the branches. The one who remains in Me and I in him bears much fruit, for [otherwise] apart from Me [that is, cut off from vital union with Me] you can do nothing."

When we are one with God, we are relying on His strength and not our own. We depend on God's wisdom and not our own. We rely on His joy and not our self-generated pleasure. We grow to know who we are through our relationship with God. We find abounding strength through intimacy (knowing, relating, and being) with God.

REFLECTION

How has God reached out to you in your lifetime? Has God communicated with you via Bible verses, song lyrics, dreams, visions, words, through a person, or a sermon?

What does the voice of God sound like to you?

What does it mean to be one with God?

PRAYER/DECLARATION

Papa God, thank you for the invitation to a relationship. Thank you for the opportunity to have a personal, intimate, and growing relationship with you. I agree with your word that I can hear your voice and know you in a profound, extraordinary way. Knowing you is a gift and the source of my strength. Help me to understand you, God.

I decree and declare that I can and do hear the voice of God. The voice of a stranger I will not follow. I can be one with God through Christ. Knowing God is the source of my strength and joy.

DAY 13:

DISCERNMENT AND TESTING ALL THINGS

Beloved, do not believe every spirit [speaking through a self-proclaimed prophet]; instead test the spirits to see whether they are from God, because many false prophets and teachers have gone out into the world. By this you know and recognize the Spirit of God: every spirit that acknowledges and confesses [the fact] that Jesus Christ has [actually] come in the flesh [as a man] is from God [God is its source]; and every spirit that does not confess Jesus [acknowledging that He has come in the flesh, but would deny any of the Son's true nature] is not of God; this is the spirit of the antichrist, which you have heard is coming, and is now already in the world. Little children (believers, dear ones), you are of God and you belong to Him and have [already] overcome them [the agents of the antichrist]; because He who is in you is greater than he (Satan) who is in the world [of sinful mankind]. (1 John 4:1-4 AMP).

DEVOTION

We live in such a culture of alternative truth and facts. If we, believers, do not know the truth of God's word and the nature of God, how will we be able to stand confidently in evil times? How will we be able to remain confident and affirm that we are hearing from God and that the information others give us is actually of God without Godly wisdom and discernment?

God tells us to test every spirit and see if it is of God. These are some standard and personal tools used to decide whether something is of God or not of God.

Is Jesus acknowledged as the Son of God? Is the deity of Christ recognized, affirmed, and stated?

Does the information align with the word of God? Study the word in context, investigate the culture and weigh the text with all of the scripture.

Does the information align with the character of God?

God is the truth.

God is love.

God is holy (there is no sin in God-God does not encourage sin).

God is faithful.

God looks out for those He loves.

God is just and fair.

God is slow to anger and abounding in love.

God is merciful and offers redemption to humans.

God is good.

God works even the unfortunate for a good outcome for those who love Him and called according to His purposes and plans. Those who forsake God, they will suffer because sin brings punishment.

God aims to lead us to repentance.

God looks out for the best interests of all involved.

God is not the author of confusion.

God is not a control freak. He allows humans to reject Him and His desires.

God does not use manipulation or control to get His way.

What is the character of the person giving the message? The Bible says we will know a tree by its fruit. What is the fruit of that person's life? Is it like God? If not, it needs to be weighed and many times tossed.

If the source is a person, does the Holy Spirit within bear witness.

Is this confirmation or something new? God loves to confirm Himself. This cannot be the only test you use.

Over the years, I have seen many people led into a ditch because they did not test what was given to them. They listened to sermons, words, dreams, pictures, impressions, and prophetic words and never tested them. They took what was said and then immediately applied it to their lives.

We do not test things because we are suffering from a spirit of suspicion. We test things because human beings see in part and know in part (1 Corinthians 13:9). Humans are not God. We are also told to test all prophecies (1 Thessalonians 5:20-21).

Deception can occur if we are not in the word and abiding in the Holy Spirit. We just do not know what we do not know. God promises to give us wisdom, understanding, and guidance if we ask of Him.

We can also grow to know the counterfeit by spending time with the original. The more we are with God, the more we will be able to recognize the imposter. Over the years, I have met people in soul healing sessions with a counterfeit Jesus and imposter Holy Spirits. They did not test the fruit of the spirits who presented themselves to them, nor the words of those spirits against the word of God.

If we pursue intimacy with God and apply some of the principles in today's devotion, we can bypass many of the traps of the enemy with deception.

REFLECTION

How do you go about testing what you hear, dream, or see? Was there something on your list that did not make it to mine?

Have you had positive experiences with the prophetic? If so, what were they? How did you know it was indeed God?

Are you applying tests to what you hear for others? If not, why not?

PRAYER/DECLARATION

Papa God, thank you for wisdom and discernment. Thank you for your word and the ability to weigh everything according to your word. Thank you for my relationship and intimacy with you. Help me to hear your voice and consider all things according to your word and character. I want to walk in your truth and not deception. Remove any and all false prophecies from my heart and mind. Help me to know what is from you and what is not from you.

I decree and declare that God is the truth. Those who worship God must worship Him in spirit and truth. I choose to align my thoughts with the thoughts of God. I have access to the wisdom of God. I have access to His truth. I decide to weigh and test things against the word of God. I declare in Christ I have access to the mind of Jesus. I invite His thoughts to be my thoughts.

DAY 14:

CONFIDENT IN THE PROMISES OF GOD

" *A*sk, *and it will be given to you; seek, and you will find; knock, and it will be opened to you. For everyone who asks receives, and he who seeks finds, and to him who knocks it will be opened. Or what man is there among you who, if his son asks for bread, will give him a stone? Or if he asks for a fish, will he give him a serpent? If you then, being evil, know how to give good gifts to your children, how much more will your Father who is in heaven give good things to those who ask Him! Therefore, whatever you want men to do to you, do also to them, for this is the Law and the Prophets. (Matthew 7:7-12 NKJV).*

DEVOTION

God is faithful to keep His word. He is also devoted to His children. There is no part of God that is evil. He is better than any earthly parent. God works for the good of His children, even in the things that are unseen. If we ask God for bread, He will not give us a stone. If we ask for fish, God will not give us a serpent. If we ask for good things, He will not provide us with something evil. God gives exceedingly, abundantly, above all we could ask or imagine (Ephesians 3:20).

We can expect the very best from God. He does not offer us scraps off the table. God comes with the very best. We can be confident that God withholds nothing good from us (Psalm 84:11).

Sometimes, we do not have the proper thing because we do not ask. Sometimes, we do not have because we murmur and complain. Sometimes, we do not have the blessing because we are not ready or have not shown the ability to be responsible. Sometimes, we do not have because what we think is right does not match God's idea of good. Sometimes in a culture, there is a push to keep up with the Joneses and the things we desire would not be beneficial in the long run. Since we see in part and know in part, only God can be trusted with all the details and to make the wisest decisions.

We have pages and pages of the Bible dedicated to the promises of God. We also have story after story of God fulfilling His promises to His children. Abraham and Sarah received their Isaac. God delivered the Israelites from the terror of Pharaoh. Hannah received her promised child. The world received the promised Messiah. Followers of Jesus received the promised Holy Spirit. These are just a few of the promises given by God and fulfilled. What God does for one, He is willing to do for another.

REFLECTION

What promises are you still waiting on from God? Have you given up or are you continuing to believe?

Do you think God wants to do exceedingly, abundantly, above all you could ask or imagine? If not, why?

Are your dreams with God getting bigger or smaller?

PRAYER/DECLARATION

Papa God, I thank you that you are faithful to your promises. I can trust you. Even when feelings and circumstances do not align with your truth, I can believe your truth. You want the very best for me. No one wants more for me than you. You are a good, good Father. Help me to believe your truth and trust you completely as Jesus did. Anything that prevents me from believing you, I ask it be uprooted and replaced with unshakable faith in your promises and character.

I decree and declare that I am blessed and favored by God as one in Christ. His will for my life is good, and He wants the very best for me. He desires to give me exceedingly, abundantly, above all I could ask or imagine. I stand confident in the promises of God and await eagerly the fulfillment of God's promises in my life.

DAY 15:

GIFTED AND INCLUDED

For by the grace [of God] given to me I say to everyone of you not to think more highly of himself [and of his importance and ability] than he ought to think; but to think so as to have sound judgment, as God has apportioned to each a degree of faith [and a purpose designed for service]. For just as in one [physical] body we have many parts, and these parts do not all have the same function or special use, so we, who are many, are [nevertheless just] one body in Christ, and individually [we are] parts one of another [mutually dependent on each other]. Since we have gifts that differ according to the grace given to us, each of us is to use them accordingly: if [someone has the gift of] prophecy, [let him speak a new message from God to His people] in proportion to the faith possessed; if service, in the act of serving; or he who teaches, in the act of teaching; or he who encourages, in the act of encouragement; he who gives, with generosity; he who leads, with diligence; he who shows mercy [in caring for others], with cheerfulness. (Romans 12:3-8 AMP).

DEVOTION

One of the most incredible parts of being connected to God is having a family. It is a global family of every tribe, tongue, and nation. It is described as a body. It is a body with many members and moving parts. Those moving parts are people who are crucial to each other. The invitation to be in God's family extends to every person who accepts Jesus as Lord, and each member given at least one gift to benefit the world.

The gifts of God come from Him. One is not limited to only do what they are naturally gifted to do. Holy Spirit is the greatest gift and has all of the spiritual gifts. If we abide in Him, we will find ourselves having numerous areas where we are gifted.

God did not leave anyone out, nor did God place a higher value on one part than another. Each person counts and each person brings something to the table that is unique, beautiful, and given to display the glory of God. Just like stained glass windows have different cut pieces of varying colors, they all fit together to create beauty. When the light shines through, there is such a glorious display. Trying to cut all the pieces the same size would be uncreative. Painting each one the same color would be equally as unexciting. God beautifully handcrafted everyone on the planet as unique expressions of who He is.

Each person has at least one gift, and we are encouraged to use each gift and talent to be a blessing to someone else. We are invited to embrace our gift(s). If we are in a state of comparison with others, we will not find joy in who we are. If we do not accept who we are, then we will miss fitting into our slot in that heavenly stained glass window. If we claim to have no gift, we do not believe God. Everything and everyone God created has a divine purpose.

REFLECTION

We can be confident that we all have something to offer, and we have a gift or gifts. What is or are your gift(s)?

Are you using these gifts to bless others?

Do you struggle with feeling included? If so, why?

What does this passage tell you about your inclusion?

PRAYER/DECLARATION

Papa God, thank you for the gifts you placed inside me. I thank you for them. Thank you for including me in your family and your plan. Thank you for handcrafting me uniquely. There is no one on earth exactly like me, and I thank you for the chance to express your creativity on this planet.

I decree and declare that I am gifted. I have something to offer; I am included in your grand plan. I am included in the ideas of God. I am created for the glory of God. I am set apart, chosen, and His handiwork. I affirm that I am accepted in the Beloved and part of the divine plan of God.

DAY 16:
FULL ACCESS GRANTED

And He raised us up together with Him [when we believed], and seated us with Him in the heavenly places, [because we are] in Christ Jesus, [and He did this] so that in the ages to come He might [clearly] show the immeasurable and unsurpassed riches of His grace in [His] kindness toward us in Christ Jesus [by providing for our redemption]. For it is by grace [God's remarkable compassion and favor drawing you to Christ] that you have been saved [actually delivered from judgment and given eternal life] through faith. And this [salvation] is not of yourselves [not through your own effort], but it is the [undeserved, gracious] gift of God; not as a result of [your] works [nor your attempts to keep the Law], so that no one will [be able to] boast or take credit in any way [for his salvation]. For we are His workmanship [His own master work, a work of art], created in Christ Jesus [reborn from above—spiritually transformed, renewed, ready to be used] for good works, which God prepared [for us] beforehand [taking paths which He set], so that we would walk in them [living the good life which He prearranged and made ready for us].

Therefore, remember that at one time you Gentiles by birth, who are called "Uncircumcision" by those who called themselves "Circumcision," [itself a mere mark] which is made in the flesh by human hands- remember that at that time you were separated from Christ [excluded from any relationship with Him], alienated from the commonwealth of Israel, and strangers to the covenants of promise [with no share in the sacred Messianic promise and without knowledge of God's agreements], having no hope [in His promise] and [living] in the world without God. But now [at this very moment] in Christ Jesus you who once were [so very] far away [from God] have been brought near by the blood of Christ. (Ephesians 2:6-13 AMP).

DEVOTION

Jesus tore the veil between humanity and God. No person could go before a holy God without being cleansed. Jesus paid the penalty for all the sins of humankind so those who believe in Him could stand before God in His righteousness. The punishment and wrath for sin were poured out on the sinless one, Jesus. He paid a debt we could not settle to reconcile us with the Father.

In Christ, we can confidently go before a loving Father without fear of death or wrath. We have secure confidence in Christ that we will be heard and loved.

God is good. If you look at other religions, you will find gods that deny access. God openly gives us access to Him through the Son. Perfect love is available and complete peace. Most importantly, we have a relationship with God. God invites us to have a personal relationship with Him. From the beginning of time, God has desired to be with humanity and dwell with us.

Not only have we been given full access to God, but we also have the invitation for oneness in Christ. He said, *"If you remain in Me and My words remain in you, ask whatever you wish, and it will be done for you,"* (John 15:7).

We can be confident in approaching God and asking anything of God.

REFLECTION

Are you confident in your ability to access God? If not, what limits you from going to God for everything?

God loves to give good gifts to His children; do you believe this truth?

What does it mean to remain in Jesus?

PRAYER/DECLARATION

Papa God, thank you for all you have done, especially giving me access to you. Thank you for your grace, mercy, and the ability to come boldly before your throne. Thank you for the covering of the blood of Jesus and the robe of His righteousness. Help me to be free of the fear of approaching you with boldness. You love me more than anyone in the world. I am safe and secure in your love.

I decree and declare that I have full access to the Father through Jesus. If I am in Christ, I wear the righteousness of God; I am no longer a stranger. I have been grafted in and have a joint inheritance with Jesus. I can approach God assertively with requests and my heart's desires. God genuinely loves me, and He longs to give me good things. The best gift He has given is a relationship with Him.

DAY 17:

EMPOWERED TO LAVISH GIVING

T*he generous man [is a source of blessing and] shall be prosperous and enriched, And he who waters will himself be watered [reaping the generosity he has sown]. (Proverbs 11:25 AMP).*

Give, and it will be given to you. They will pour into your lap a good measure—pressed down, shaken together, and running over [with no space left for more]. For with the standard of measurement you use [when you do good to others], it will be measured to you in return." (Luke 6:38 AMP).

Heal the sick, raise the dead, cleanse the lepers, cast out demons. Freely you have received, freely give. (Matthew 10:8 AMP).

DEVOTION

There is such a blessing tied to genuine generosity. God is love, and the right nature of love is giving. Love looks out for the best interests of others. Love gives unselfishly.

One of the reasons God blesses us is so we can be a blessing to others. We are to be conduits of the goodness of God.

When we connect with the heart of God, there is an increased desire to bless others. As we abide in God's love, our focus moves from solely inward focus to outward focus.

God is 100% good; "Every good and perfect gift is from above, coming down from the Father of the heavenly lights, with whom there is no change or shifting shadow," James 1:17 (Berean Study Bible). As we soak and abide in who God is, we become full to overflowing with goodness to share with the world. Intimacy with God, knowing Him, taps us into the source of kindness, love, and blessings that does not run dry.

There is confidence that arises when we can express the same love for others that God has for us. As we soak in God's love and goodness, there is a wealth of God's love to give away. It is not about what that person can do for us; it is about what God has already done for us.

There is confidence found in loving others without being devastated by the lack of reciprocation. It's not about what others can do for us. It is about who we are in God. We allow God to love us deeply and thoroughly, then we operate out of the overflow.

REFLECTION

God gave it all for us, who are you investing in and where are you sowing lavishly?

Why do you think God says it is better to give rather than receive?

What motivates you to give?

What causes you to want to shrink back from giving?

PRAYER/DECLARATION

Papa God, thank you for all you have given me. You freely offered up your Son to us and gave us access to you. You seated us in heavenly places and gave us every spiritual blessing in the heavenly places in Christ. Thank you. I ask that the same love you have demonstrated for me would be given away. Help me to be a generous person, someone who is known for radical generosity and for being kind to others. Saturate my heart with your steadfast and incredible love.

I decree and declare my life is marked and led by radical generosity. I have a heart to share and to give. As I give, more is given unto me so that I can pour out more to others. My legacy with God will be love. Love unselfishly gives; therefore, I am a cheerful giver. I declare a life of confidence in giving.

DAY 18:

CONFIDENCE WHEN FACING REJECTION

Blessed and worthy of praise be the God and Father of our Lord Jesus Christ, who has blessed us with every spiritual blessing in the heavenly realms in Christ, just as [in His love] He chose us in Christ [actually selected us for Himself as His own] before the foundation of the world, so that we would be holy [that is, consecrated, set apart for Him, purpose-driven] and blameless in His sight. In love He predestined and lovingly planned for us to be adopted to Himself as [His own] children through Jesus Christ, in accordance with the kind intention and good pleasure of His will—to the praise of His glorious grace and favor, which He so freely bestowed on us in the Beloved [His Son, Jesus Christ]. (Ephesians 1:3-6 AMP).

DEVOTION

Rejection is something most people will face at some point in time in life. There are two quotes I love. One says, *"No one can make you feel inferior without your consent,"* Eleanor Roosevelt. The other is, *"You can be the juiciest peach in the world, and there will still be someone who does not like peaches."*

Humans have the incredible ability to choose. Love involves the freedom to choose. The ability to choose is a gift. Sometimes, it is painful not to be selected. It can be painful to be overlooked, cast aside, and left out. The good news is that God does not leave us out. God does not throw us aside. God stands in great love for us. God does not mistreat us. God's hand-selected us before the foundations of the earth to be accepted in the Beloved, His most precious Son. Overlooked by humanity does not mean God ignores a person.

King David was rejected by those in his family, and he became a king. Joseph was rejected and sold into slavery by his brothers, and he was promoted to lead a nation. We read story after story of people in the Bible overlooked and rejected by humans and elevated by God.

Sometimes rejection is God's protection. God knows what is best and wants the very best for us. He will allow us to be overlooked by those who will not love us or care for us the way He does. It is wise not to chase after those that God allows removed. Sometimes those who leave are a blessing in disguise.

Rejection can also be perceived; that person may not have received that message, that gift may have been lost in the mail, that person may be led to do something different other than what is asked of them, or that person may not be ready for a relationship.

The love of God and knowing who we are in Christ are the cures for rejection. We were created to be loved and not rejected. Since humanity fell and all do not abide in perfect love, there is rejection. We can be confident if we are in Christ and following Jesus, we will not be rejected by God.

REFLECTION

Is there a lingering rejection that is still hurting your heart? If so, invite God into that situation. Ask God for His eyes for what happened.

How can accepting God's love change the way you view rejection? (Hint: being rejected by humankind does not mean rejected by God).

Have you ever rejected someone or something? Did you think about the impact on the other person?

PRAYER/DECLARATION

Papa, I thank you that in Christ, I am accepted in the Beloved. I am not rejected. I am deeply loved. I invite you into every single soul wound to heal and restore. Where there is a wound, bring your comfort. Where the enemy has sown lies, reveal every single one, so they are renounced, and I can come out of agreement with every lie. Saturate my heart and soul with your truth.

I decree and declare that I am loved. I refute all lies of rejection and forgive any person who made me feel rejected. I claim freedom for my soul from wounds of rejection. I am confident in who God created me to be. I am free to be who God created me to be and live loved. Even if I am ignored by people, I am never overlooked by God.

BONUS (Soul Healing for Rejection)

The following activation is designed to help access soul wounds from rejection and lies believed based on rejection.

Activation prayer: Holy Spirit I invite you to search my heart and soul for wounds from rejection. Please reveal any lies I have come into agreement with based on rejection.

Get quiet and listen. As you listen, jot down anything that comes to mind. It may sound like, "No one loves me," or "I am always rejected," or "I am unworthy of love."

Once you have your list, walk through the following prayer and renounce every lie.

In the name of Jesus, I renounce the lie (insert lie) and come out of agreement with this lie (insert lie). I command every spirit that came to reinforce this lie to leave me and go to Jesus. Do not return to me. Holy Spirit flood my soul with your love, truth, purity, goodness, and acceptance. Help me to accept myself, and love myself the way you do. I repent for believing lies about myself and humbly accept your truth.

Some rejections run deep. They require deep inner healing. God is the healer, and we will jump into healing the soul more on day 19.

DAY 19:

HEALED AND WHOLE IN THE SOUL

Beloved, I pray that you may prosper in all things and be in health, just as your soul prospers. (3 John 2:2 NKJV).

But He was wounded for our transgressions, He was bruised for our iniquities; The chastisement for our peace was upon Him, and by His stripes, we are healed. (Isaiah 53:5 NKJV).

DEVOTION

We are triune beings comprised of a body, spirit, and soul. Pain in one area can cause pain in other areas.

Whole regeneration of our spirit is complete at conversion (2 Corinthians 5:17). The soul consists of the mind, will, and emotions. The mind, will, and emotions are to yield to and be transformed by the Holy Spirit.

Our souls are being sanctified; minds are to be renewed (Romans 12:2), emotions expressed with self-control (Ephesians 4:26), and our will must submit to God's will (James 4:7). These things in our souls are not automatically changed into the likeness of Jesus.

God's heart is to heal the entire person; mind, body, and soul.

Soul health is essential to overall health. If the soul is wounded, decisions can be challenging. Emotions (feelings) can drive actions instead of the Holy Spirit. Decisions made by emotions can be destructive and lead to regret.

Soul wounds not healed can also cloud perceptions. It's like looking through broken glasses. A soul carrying pain, rejection, unforgiveness, abandonment, lust, greed, selfishness, and (fill in things that are not like God) can cause problems in all areas of life.

Negative thoughts lead to negative emotions which can lead to negative behaviors.

Just as Jesus healed the body, He heals the soul. If we invite God into the wounded parts of our souls, we can find healing and wholeness in God. God enters the most wounded parts of our souls and interjects light to cast out negative thoughts/emotions. God brings wholeness.

Some wounds were created in the womb (unwantedness, abandonment, fear, rejection) and some later in life when our coping mechanisms are low. These wounds need to be healed by Jesus.

Soul healing begins with God.

REFLECTION

Are there places in your heart, emotions that are out of alignment with God? (Examples: Anger, rage, fear, lust, road rage, lying, rejection, self-condemnation).

What promise has God given concerning healing?

PRAYER/DECLARATION

My soul is being made whole by the power and love of God. I am made whole by His love, peace, joy, provision, and strength. I have access to perfect health. Jesus paid for the healing and restoration of my entire soul.

Papa God, thank you for uniting me with Christ. Thank you for all He paid for on the cross including the healing of my soul and mind. I thank you for access to healing. I ask that your Holy Spirit would saturate my soul in your peace, love, power, acceptance, and joy. Every place where there has been pain or darkness, I ask for a release of your light. You are pure love and pure light. Let that light invade my entire being. In Jesus mighty name, Amen.

DAY 20:

CONFIDENT IN FRIENDSHIP WITH GOD

" "This is My commandment, that you love and unselfishly seek the best for one another, just as I have loved you. No one has greater love [nor stronger commitment] than to lay down his own life for his friends. You are my friends if you keep on doing what I command you. I do not call you servants any longer, for the servant does not know what his master is doing; but I have called you [My] friends, because I have revealed to you everything that I have heard from My Father. You have not chosen Me, but I have chosen you, and I have appointed and placed and purposefully planted you, so that you would go and bear fruit and keep on bearing, and that your fruit will remain and be lasting, so that whatever you ask of the Father in My name [as My representative] He may give to you. This [is what] I command you: that you love and unselfishly seek the best for one another. (John 15:12-17 AMP).

DEVOTION

Jesus gave an incredible command to the disciples concerning love. It was a love that was first demonstrated by Him to the disciples. This love was the love Jesus shared with the Father. He gives an incredible promise of love and friendship not slavery to His followers.

In John 15:13-15 Jesus tells us that there is no greater love a person has than to lay down his or her life for their friends. It is agape love (perfect, unselfish, and sacrificial love). This love was demonstrated for humanity before they knew Him. God invites us to be His friends. It is a friendship that does not negate or diminish His Lordship, nor does it mean we treat God as casual. It does say that we have access to God that was once denied based on the sinfulness of humanity. What once separated us from God was taken care of by the Son. So, we can be confident in our connection with God if we are in Christ.

Jesus describes being with Him as following His commands and receiving what He reveals. Friends share intimacy. Intimacy (knowing, bonding, and connection) is what God wanted from the beginning. In the Garden of Eden, God wanted a relationship with humanity. Jesus made this possible by taking our sin and clothing us in His righteousness.

Friendship means we can approach God with the confidence of God's love for us. No matter what we have done, we can know the heart of God is to forgive and reconcile. God promises to be the friend that sticks closer than a brother (Proverbs 18:24). God promises to be the friend who will never betray us, be too busy for us, neglects us, or hurts us. What better friend could we ask for in life? The friendship with God is eternal and perfect.

REFLECTION

What does the word friend mean to you?

Who is your best friend and why?

What does it mean to have God as a friend?

PRAYER/DECLARATION

Papa God, thank you for blessing me with the friendship of Jesus. Thank you for your friendship and the friendship of the Holy Spirit. Deepen our friendship. I want to know you and know more about you. I ask that you deepen my awareness of your love and our connection.

I decree and declare that I am a friend of God. In Christ, I have been given full access to God. I have a friend that sticks closer than a brother, and I am never alone or without a true friend. I am secure in the friendship of God.

DAY 21:
CONFIDENT IN CRISIS

*A*t that time certain Chaldeans came forward and brought [malicious] accusations against the Jews. They said to King Nebuchadnezzar, "O king, live forever! You, O king, have made a decree that everyone who hears the sound of the horn, pipe, lyre, trigon, harp, dulcimer, bagpipe, and all kinds of music is to fall down and worship the golden image. Whoever does not fall down and worship shall be thrown into the midst of a furnace of blazing fire. There are certain Jews whom you have appointed over the administration of the province of Babylon, namely Shadrach, Meshach, and Abednego. These men, O king, pay no attention to you; they do not serve your gods or worship the golden image which you have set up."

Then Nebuchadnezzar in a furious rage gave a command to bring Shadrach, Meshach, and Abednego; and these men were brought before the king. Nebuchadnezzar said to them, "Is it true, Shadrach, Meshach, and Abednego, that you do not serve my gods or worship the golden image which I have set up? Now if you are ready, when you

85

hear the sound of the horn, pipe, lyre, trigon, harp, dulcimer, and all kinds of music, to fall down and worship the image which I have made, very good. But if you do not worship, you shall be thrown at once into the midst of a furnace of blazing fire; and what god is there who can rescue you out of my hands?"

Shadrach, Meshach, and Abednego answered the king, "O Nebuchadnezzar, we do not need to answer you on this point. If it be so, our God whom we serve is able to rescue us from the furnace of blazing fire, and He will rescue us from your hand, O king. But even if He does not, let it be known to you, O king, that we are not going to serve your gods or worship the golden image that you have set up!"

Daniel's Friends Protected

Then Nebuchadnezzar was filled with fury, and his facial expression changed toward Shadrach, Meshach, and Abednego. Then he gave a command that the furnace was to be heated seven times hotter than usual. He commanded certain strong men in his army to tie up Shadrach, Meshach, and Abednego and to throw them into the furnace of blazing fire. Then these [three] men were tied up in their trousers, their coats, their turbans, and their other clothes, and were thrown into the midst of the furnace of blazing fire. Because the king's command was urgent and the furnace was extremely hot, the flame of the fire killed the men who carried up Shadrach, Meshach, and Abednego. But these three men, Shadrach, Meshach, and Abednego, fell into the midst of the furnace of blazing fire still tied up.

Then Nebuchadnezzar the king [looked and] was astounded, and he jumped up and said to his counselors, "Did we not throw three men who were tied up into the midst of the fire?" They replied to the king, "Certainly, O king." He answered, "Look! I see four men untied, walking around in the midst of the fire, and they are not hurt! And the appearance of the fourth is like a son of the gods!" Then Nebuchadnezzar approached the door of the blazing furnace and said, "Shadrach, Meshach, and Abednego, servants of the Most High God, come out [of there]! Come here!" Then Shadrach, Meshach, and Abednego came out of the midst of the fire. The satraps, the prefects, the governors and the king's counselors gathered around them and saw that in regard to these men the fire had no effect on their bodies—their hair was not singed, their clothes were not scorched or damaged, even the smell of smoke was not on them (Daniel 3:8-27).

DEVOTION

Life will present us with adversity and challenges. Life may even give us a crisis or series of crisis events. How we respond in those times of pain, problems, and uncertainty will determine whether we have a more profound or weaker connection with God.

Adversity and challenges can bond us or be detrimental to a relationship. We see this when tragedy strikes our hometown or country. People who usually would not speak to one another, nor have any connection, all of a sudden bond and connect. There is the confidence that you and I can and will get through this together.

God revealed His care and power to Shadrach, Meshach, and Abednego in the midst of adverse circumstances. The men understood that even if they were not delivered from their circumstances, God was still God. God remains good, powerful, and love even in the midst of our crisis.

Shadrach, Meshach, and Abednego refused to lose heart or abandon their faith in the midst of a crisis. They should have been consumed in the fire that was turned up 7 times hotter, yet they were not consumed. They came out and did not smell like smoke.

The experiences of other's overcoming and the examination of our previous seasons overcoming challenges can build trust for the next. We are to look at the success of God in the past as a stepping stone for the future. Recall what God has done. Recall who God is. They had Jesus on board. Therefore, there was no need to fear.

If we are in Christ, we too have God with us. He is not sleeping in another room; He is living on the inside of us. The same power that raised Christ from the dead lives on the inside of us (Romans 8:11). It is not a little light or a small amount of power. It is the same power that raised Jesus. It is not weak, incapable, nor withholding. God longs to display His strength in our weakness.

When crisis raises its ugly head, we have an Advocate on the inside of us ready to respond with His peace. The peace comes in the presence of God. The winds and the waves must still obey God. The fires of life are not stronger than God. One word from the mouth of God changes everything. One thing we can do in the crisis and fires of life, is to pursue intimacy with God and say, "Lord, what should be my response to the situation? What is your insight? I am listening and waiting for a word from you."

All of my parents have had health issues. I recall over and over crying out to God in crisis. Sometimes the peace came with one small sentence from God, "I am here, and I am going to take care of your parents." It's His voice, His presence, and strength that fortifies us in the midst of storms and crisis. More than anything, we can be confident that God is with us and wants the best for us. Even when the crisis is self-inflicted, we can call on Jesus to help us. His perfect love for us does not fail.

REFLECTION

What is your first response to a crisis?

Who is the first person you contact in the midst of a crisis or challenge? Is it God? If so, how has that helped you? If not, who is your go-to person and why?

What is the lesson taught by God to the boys in the fiery furnace in the midst of their crisis?

PRAYER/DECLARATION

Papa God, thank you for your steadfast love. Thank you for watching over me in calm seas and raging storms. Thank you for being there in every season. I repent of any unbelief and not trusting in your ability to care for me at all times. Help me to turn to you during times of pain, uncertainty, and crisis. Those who place their trust in you will never be disappointed.

Nothing can separate me from the love of God in Christ Jesus. His will for me is always good. He wants the best for me. I can trust His sovereignty and protection over my life. Jesus came that I may have life and have it to the fullest.

DAY 22:
CONFIDENT WITHOUT
PERFECTION

I n Him also we have [received an inheritance [a destiny—we were claimed by God as His own], having been predestined (chosen, appointed beforehand) according to the purpose of Him who works everything in agreement with the counsel and design of His will, so that we who were the first to hope in Christ [who first put our confidence in Him as our Lord and Savior] would exist to the praise of His glory. In Him, you also, when you heard the word of truth, the good news of your salvation, and [as a result] believed in Him, were stamped with the seal of the promised Holy Spirit [the One promised by Christ] as owned and protected [by God]. The Spirit is the guarantee [the first installment, the pledge, a foretaste] of our inheritance until the redemption of God's own [purchased] possession [His believers], to the praise of His glory. (Ephesians 1:11-14 AMP).

DEVOTION

God knew us before we ever said yes to Him. God knew all of the quirks and imperfections. God knew our weaknesses and remained steadfast in the choice to choose us. We were hand selected by God to be loved, recognized, and adopted into His family.

There is nothing hidden from God. We do not need to hide like Adam and Eve in the garden. We can stand confident that we are loved despite imperfections. Our imperfections are not who we are; they are not our true identity. If we are united with Jesus, our true identity is son or daughter of God.

Over the years, I have heard so many people put themselves down, focus on their imperfections, and not have the joy of God because of hyper-focus on what needs growth. God focuses on loving us right where we are; yielding to His love promotes growth.

I had these plants on my sun porch. The seed went deep into the soil, and I did not see that seed again. I watered my seed, and then I noticed it grew towards the light. Some vines grew twisted, or weeds grew to choke out my plant. I, as the gardener, would prune the plant to produce the most fruit. The plant focused on the light. I provided the pruning and growth opportunities.

In our lives, God is the Master Gardener, and we are the plants. We are to focus on the Light (God), yield to God's pruning (wisdom, instruction, guidance), and grow. The gardener is not hyper-focused on the imperfections; the goal is the health of the plant. God wants us to be healthy and thrive.

You and I can rest in the goodness of God. We can focus on God and release our imperfections to God, the Master Gardener. We can focus on His Light (love and truth) and love ourselves the way God does. The critical thing to note is we were chosen by love (God) before we were ever set free and following Jesus. The love of God is a love that frees us to love ourselves and stand as confident children of God.

REFLECTION

Do you tend to focus more on your strengths or your weaknesses? Based on your answer which is more beneficial?

Do you think God is more focused on your strengths or your weaknesses? Why do you think or feel this way?

How does knowing God loved you before you even said yes to Him change the way you view His acceptance of you?

PRAYER/DECLARATION

Papa God, thank you for your unfailing love. Thank you for loving me first. Thank you for pursuing me with your steadfast love. Thank you for seeing my imperfections and flaws and choosing me. I am adopted and accepted in the beloved. Help me to remain confident in who I am in you. Help me to focus more on what you say than to focus on my thoughts or the thoughts of others.

I am entirely accepted by God through my relationship with Jesus. I am accepted in the beloved. The love God freely has for me is the same love I am to receive for myself. I am loved for who I am not where I will be. I love and accept myself the way God does in the Son.

DAY 23:

FREEDOM FROM SHAME

*I*nstead of your [former] shame, you will have a [double portion; And instead of humiliation, your people will shout for joy over their portion. Therefore, in their land, they will possess double [what they had forfeited];Everlasting joy will be theirs. For I, the Lord, love justice; I hate robbery with a burnt offering. And I will faithfully reward them, And make an everlasting covenant with them. (Isaiah 61:7-8 AMP).

DEVOTION

First, I would love to define shame. It is a word that is sometimes confused with conviction. Webster's dictionary defines shame as, "a condition of humiliating disgrace or disrepute." Shame is also a negative emotion that causes us to hide, shrink back, feel rejected, and unloved. Shame is a powerful emotion. Shame not surrendered to God can cripple us. Shame caused Adam and Eve to hide from God in the Garden. The God they knew who walked in the cool of the day in the Garden of Eden became someone to protect themselves from, and then blame others for their choices.

Shame does not lead to a beautiful outcome. It is an enemy of intimacy (knowing) with God. Shame attempts to distort identity. Instead of simply running to God and saying, "I did something outside your will," shame brings with it an identity change, "I am what I did."

Godly conviction says, "I stepped outside of my identity as a son or daughter of God. What I did, or thought does not reflect my true identity. I will repent (realign my thoughts with God) and course correct to reflect who I truly am. I am created in the image of God." Shame says, "Because I have done or thought something unlike God, I am a horrible person. My identity has changed to the sin I committed."

God wants to free us from shame. Conviction shines the light on a thought or behavior to see repentance and restoration. Shame seeks to cause fear, insecurity, and a change in the area of identity.

The bible says, "As a person thinketh in their heart so are they," Proverbs 23:7. When sin becomes our identity, we begin to act out what we believe. A person who struggles with anger becomes an angry person. Once that becomes their identity, most will find they are angry and continue to be angry. The same person who says, "My identity is a child of God, and though I may struggle, this is not my identity," may find out that they have an easier time being free from anger.

God wants us to draw near during times of weakness instead of running away and hiding from Him. God wants us to be confident that no matter what we have done or what has been done to us, our true identity is in Him. We are who God says that we are.

REFLECTION

How do you define shame and conviction?

Is part of your identity determined by what you have done or what has been done to you?

Who does God say that you are?

PRAYER/DECLARATION

Papa God, thank you for taking my shame away and providing freedom in Jesus. Those who the Son sets free are free indeed. I am choosing today to come out of the partnership with the spirit of shame. I am deeply loved and accepted in the beloved. I renounce humiliation, rejection, and self-rejection and command any spirits not the Holy Spirit to leave me and go to Jesus. I choose to accept the truth of your word. I am loved.

I am who God says that I am. My mistakes do not define me, nor the weaknesses, or the things that have been done to me. I am established by what God says. Only the opinion of God matters. My identity, if I am in Christ, is a child of God. I am seated in heavenly places with His Son Jesus and accepted in the beloved. For my former shame and disgrace, God will give me double honor.

DAY 24:

ACCESS TO THE CONTENTMENT OF GOD

Not that I speak from [any personal] need, for I have learned to be content [and self-sufficient through Christ, satisfied to the point where I am not disturbed or uneasy] regardless of my circumstances. I know how to get along and live humbly [in difficult times], and I also know how to enjoy abundance and live in prosperity. In any and every circumstance, I have learned the secret [of facing life], whether well-fed or going hungry, whether having an abundance or being in need. I can do all things [which He has called me to do] through Him who strengthens and empowers me [to fulfill His purpose—I am self-sufficient in Christ's sufficiency; I am ready for anything and equal to anything through Him who infuses me with inner strength and confident peace.] (Philippians 4:11-13 AMP).

DEVOTION

The one who has learned contentment in Christ is truly free. Being discontent is a form of bondage. It is a temporary or permanent state of discontentment. It is void of lasting joy. Joy is not about what is happening. Joy exists in the presence of Jesus. Happiness is based on what is happening to us, and whether things are going the way we would like them to go. Joy is a fruit of the Holy Spirit and God with us is the most genuine freedom.

Paul wrote many of His letters from jail or house arrest. Each greeting had threads of hope and thankfulness for the person of Jesus or expressed gratitude for his letter audience. There was remarkable contentment in the life of Apostle Paul. He had such a powerful encounter with God on the road to Damascus. He was changed forever by an encounter with God. Intimacy with God was the hallmark of his life post encounter with Jesus.

Knowing God and the goodness of God opens us up to a new level of contentment. It does not mean there will not be things we wish to see changed in our lives, in our world, or in the lives of those around us. It does indicate we can see with the eyes of God that no matter where we are, and no matter what occurs, there is One higher. Our eyes move from the temporal to the eternal.

Contentment is not, "I am in this horrible situation, and I love it." Contentment is, "I am in this challenging situation, and God is here. I love God." Without God, there can be no true and lasting peace. Jesus stated very plainly, "I have told you these things, so that in Me you may have [perfect] peace. In the world, you have tribulation and distress and suffering, but be courageous [be confident, be undaunted, be filled with joy]; I have overcome the world." [My conquest is accomplished, My victory abiding.]," (John 16:33 AMP).

The Victor (Jesus) has come, and He empowers us through His Spirit to overcome.

Paul stated something that bears repeating, "God infuses me with inner strength and confident peace." It is not about our abilities to be content. It is and has always been about the presence of God and His strength.

REFLECTION

List off any areas of your life where there is or has been discontentment and dissatisfaction.

Have you invited God into those areas?

Have you asked God to infuse you with His strength to be content in those areas?

What promises has God given to provide comfort in uncomfortable situations? (Hints: Matthew 28:20, Deuteronomy 31:6, Hebrews 13:5, John 10:10, Psalm 84:11, John 14:2-3). Look up these verses and commit them to memory.

PRAYER/DECLARATION

Papa God, I thank you for being with me in every situation. I am never alone nor without hope. You are my infuser of strength and confident peace. Therefore, I can be content with you regardless of my circumstances. I can be assured that you are working all things together for an overarching good. You can be trusted. Help me to place trust firmly in you. Heal every place in me that created a soul wound that enables unbelief and discontentment. In Jesus mighty name, Amen.

God has exceptional plans for my life. I can be confident that He who began a good work in and around me will complete what He started. I am blessed. My most divine blessing is God; therefore, I will rejoice in the presence of God. I have a sure hope, and that is Jesus. No matter my circumstances, I will hold fast to God's unwavering truth.

DAY 25:

FREEDOM FROM TRAUMA

*T*hen they cried out to the Lord in their trouble,
And He saved them out of their distresses.
He sent His word and healed them,
And delivered them from their destructions.
Oh, that men would give thanks to the Lord for His goodness,
And for His wonderful works to the children of men!
(Psalm 107:19-21 NKJV).

DEVOTION

Trauma is something that can bind us. It is a form of injury to the body and soul. Many things can cause shock or damage to the soul, spirit, and body. Persecution, car accidents, abuse, rejection, abandonment, racism, sexism, surgeries, prolonged sickness, betrayal, bullying, and oppression can cause trauma to the body and soul.

There are cases of people who endured great affliction, oppression, and persecution who later became ill in their body because there was trauma in the soul.

What is trauma?

Trauma is, according to dictionary.com:

1. a deeply distressing or disturbing experience.
2. physical injury.

Sometimes, the trauma brings in fear, anxiety, rejection, offense, unforgiveness (towards self or those who created the wound), or infirmity (sickness/disease). Trauma can also distort the view of God or ourselves. Trauma can rob us of confidence in who we are, and who God is to us.

The psalmist tells us that God works on behalf of the oppressed and distressed. God is the deliverer and freer of the captives.

Trauma is not supposed to be our life or life story. Regardless of what has happened to us, God invites us to find freedom in Him and health. Out of God's lovingkindness, God moves on behalf of the hurting.

God cares about what happens to us. He cares about every single detail. Though God does not prevent all trauma (sin and human free will gives us trouble on earth), God does provide healing for the injuries we face. It can be challenging to see God's goodness and love when a trauma comes. Where was God? Why did God allow this to happen? Why am I going through this traumatic experience? I can only speak what I know of God and His word.

I learned God does not approve of any sin, so the injustices against us were not His idea. The thief comes to steal, kill, and destroy. Jesus came to give us life and life to the fullest. Things that come to rob us of life, love, peace, and joy are not from God. God wants us to prosper and be in health even as our soul prospers (3 John 2).

REFLECTION

Have you experienced a trauma? If so, did it change your view of yourself or God?

Have you suffered any physical impairment based on your trauma?

How does knowing that God wants you to be blessed and not traumatized impact your thoughts?

PRAYER/DECLARATION

Papa God, thank you for seeing me through my traumatic experiences. I ask for deep inner healing and total restoration of my soul. I desire the appropriation for all Jesus paid for on the cross for me. He paid for healing and deliverance, and I want that fully appropriated to every part of my life. Flood my soul with your love, peace, joy, healing, and goodness. I break the curses of trauma, infirmity, and oppression attached to my soul from my traumatic experiences. I command any spirit that is not the Holy Spirit to leave me and to go to Jesus. Do not ever return to me. Holy Spirit clean out every soul wound bearing trauma. In Jesus mighty name Amen.

My soul was created to be whole and filled with the light, love, peace, and joy of God. Jesus paid to free me from all trauma. I decree and declare that those the Son sets free are free indeed. I can trust God to heal, restore, and transform my soul, so it aligns with heaven. I declare freedom in my soul.

BONUS (Soul Healing from Trauma)

Trauma in the soul does not bring about a prosperous life. Let's get rid of trauma. You will need a pen and paper. You will also need to devote some time to do this activity.

105

ACTIVATION

I severe between soul and spirit. Any spirit attached to wounds on my soul, I command you to be bound until sent to Jesus. Holy Spirit, I invite you to wash over my soul and reveal any entry points of trauma and the negative emotions attached to those wounds.

Listen to what the Holy Spirit brings to mind. It may come as an impression, picture, date, or memory recall. Write down the information that comes to mind. An example may be that you were in a car accident at age 7, and the negative emotions brought to mind are fear, dread, fear of not being in control, anger, sadness, pain, and grief. Ask the Holy Spirit to reveal all wounds, then say the following prayer.

God, thank you for revealing wounds on my soul. I want them healed. I invite Jesus into every single place that hurts to demonstrate His truth, love, and goodness.

Wait and allow Jesus to minister to the wounded places. You may cry or feel some of the emotions you felt at the time of trauma. Ask Jesus to take the negative emotions away and show you or tell you where He was during the incidents. Once you have been ministered to by Jesus, pray the following.

In the name of Jesus and by the authority given in His name, I break the curse of trauma, pain, grief, infirmity, sickness, and (insert all negative emotions revealed). I command any and all spirits, that are not the Holy Spirit that came and attached to this wound to leave me and go to Jesus. Holy Spirit, fill every place where the enemy has been with your love, life, purity, goodness, joy, and truth. Bring wholeness to my entire soul.

DAY 26:

FREEDOM FROM THE OPINIONS

OF MAN (PEOPLE PLEASING)

T *he fear of man brings a snare, but whoever trusts in and puts his confidence in the Lord will be exalted and safe. (Proverbs 29:25 AMP).*

Out of my distress I called on the Lord;
The Lord answered me and set me free.
The Lord is on my side; I will not fear.
What can [mere] man do to me?
The Lord is on my side, He is among those who help me;
Therefore I will look [in triumph] on those who hate me. (Psalm 118:5-7 AMP).

DEVOTION

The fear of man, caring what people think is a trap. It places people above God to be the one who provides approval. The issue with people-pleasing is it is fear based; it is fear of rejection. If we do not gain the support of others, then there is the potential for rejection. God invites us to care more about what He thinks that the opinions of others (man).

When we need the approval of others, they become a God-substitute for us. We bend and move based on their opinions instead of listening to the words of God. People pleasing and caring what others think robs us of godly confidence. People can change their minds and ideas just based on their feelings or experiences. God does not change.

Have you ever had someone claim to love you deeply, then change their mind, and you never heard from them again? I have. Therefore, I choose not to base my self-worth or confidence on the opinions of people. I understand their thoughts of me can swiftly change. They can also, if not rooted in the word of God and Spirit of God, lead us to paths that are not of God.

Our confidence must be in God; who God is, what God has done, and who God says we are. The demands of people did not dictate the life of Jesus. Jesus moved according to the will of the Father. His identity was quite secure in who He was as the Son of God. He could say no, set boundaries, and move about doing what He saw the Father doing and saying what He heard the Father saying.

Jesus, though popular today, was not loved by everyone. His willingness to only do the will of the Father led people to want Him dead. People persecuted Jesus for His obedience to the Father's will. Yet, the Father gave Jesus the name above all names and seated Him at His right hand.

The applause of heaven is always more important than the praise of people. People do not decide our eternal fate, eternal rewards, nor can people genuinely validate us. At the end of our lives, God will not hold a committee of our peers to talk about our eternal fate. God alone will decide our fate. So, we can be free from living bound to pleasing people. We can be confident of who we are in Christ and seek to please God alone.

REFLECTION

Do you struggle with people pleasing? If so, how does bending to the desires of people impact your life?

Who does God say should be elevated and first in our lives?

How does people-pleasing impact your confidence?

PRAYER/DECLARATION

Papa God, thank you that I am free from the slavery of people-pleasing. I have in you the ability to be confident to do your will and not be tossed around by a desire to please everyone else. Help me to be a God chaser and not a chaser of the approval of man which is not stable. I ask for total freedom from fear of man and caring what people think about me. What you think about me matters more than anything. I repent for idolatry (caring more what people think than you). Keep my heart free from idols. In Jesus mighty name, Amen.

The only opinion that truly matters in my life is that of God. I am free to be who I am in Christ, free to say no, and able to set boundaries. I am not bound to the pulling and tugging of people. I am to follow Jesus and to do what is honoring to Him. My eternal security is in Christ and not the commentary of people.

DAY 27:

FREEDOM TO UNDERSTAND SPIRITUAL THINGS

Now we have received, not the spirit of the world, but the [Holy] Spirit who is from God, so that we may know and understand the [wonderful] things freely given to us by God. We also speak of these things, not in words taught or supplied by human wisdom, but in those taught by the Spirit, combining and interpreting spiritual thoughts with spiritual words [for those being guided by the Holy Spirit].

But the natural [unbelieving] man does not accept the things [the teachings and revelations] of the Spirit of God, for they are foolishness [absurd and illogical] to him; and he is incapable of understanding them, because they are spiritually discerned and appreciated, [and he is unqualified to judge spiritual matters]. But the spiritual man [the spiritually mature Christian] judges all things [questions, examines and applies what the Holy Spirit reveals], yet is himself judged by no one [the unbeliever cannot judge and understand the believer's spiritual nature]. For who has known the mind and purposes of the Lord, so as *to instruct Him? But we have the mind of Christ [to be guided by His thoughts and purposes]. (1 Corinthians 2:12-16 AMP).*

DEVOTION

The mind of the unregenerate man (the person who has not given his life to Jesus) struggles and cannot understand spiritual things. The sinful become frustrated or irate in their conversations with those in a relationship with Jesus. There seems to be a disconnect between realities.

One of the blessings of being in Christ is the ability to have a revelation from the Holy Spirit. Holy Spirit is fully God and a teacher of the heart, will, nature, character, and words of Jesus and the Father. Those in Christ can ask God for wisdom and to have the revelation of God given to them. It is a blessing to be able to hear from God and to understand God.

Having access to the mind of Christ means there are spiritual concepts and insights open to us that would not be available otherwise. The Bible is clear that whosoever should need wisdom should inquire of God who gives wisdom liberally (James 1:5). The knowledge and understanding of God are available to believers.

There are heavenly downloads available to those in Christ who pursue God. Intimacy with God is the seed planting place of revelation. Just as two human beings grow to know each other via closeness and communication, we grow in wisdom through intimacy with God. Revelation is a fruit of intimacy.

We can grow in confidence that we hear from God by being rooted in His word, testing things we hear, and studying God's character.

Part of intimacy and understanding spiritual things flows through inviting God into our study of His word. The book (the Bible) does not replace experiences with God. We need both. The Bible is to lead us into an encounter with God; it is not just a textbook to study to grow in intellectual understanding and spiritual insight.

Think of something you did not understand before, yet, someone came along and taught you. God sent His Holy Spirit to be the come-beside-us and live-inside-us teacher. He comes to reveal and guide us from the inside. The regeneration of the spirit at conversion (giving our lives to God) provides us with the capability to understand the things of God.

REFLECTION

Do you believe you hear from God and have the ability to understand spiritual concepts? If so, why? If not, why not?

After reading today's devotion, has your confidence grown that you are wired to understand spiritual truths?

Do you rely on Holy Spirit or your own understanding to know God and His truths? Which has been more fruitful?

PRAYER/DECLARATION

Papa God, thank you for salvation and the ability to renew my mind. Help me to seek you for wisdom, your truth, and your insight. Help me not to lean on my own understanding. Fill me to overflowing with confidence that I hear from you. I can read and understand your word by the power and revelation of the Holy Spirit. Remove any deception and replace it with your truth. Holy Spirit, teach me your ways. In Jesus mighty name, Amen.

I can know God and understand His truths. I have access to the mind of Christ. My spirit was regenerated, and therefore I have access to the wisdom, insight of God. I can be confident that the Holy Spirit will teach me the words and will of God. My desire is for the truth of God and for His truth to permeate my entire being.

DAY 28:

FREEDOM TO REST

I*n peace [and with a tranquil heart] I will both lie down and sleep, For You alone, O Lord, make me dwell in safety and confident trust. (Psalm 4:8 AMP). For God alone my soul waits in silence; From Him comes my salvation. He alone is my rock and my salvation. My defense and my strong tower; I will not be shaken or disheartened. (Psalm 62:1-2 AMP).*

DEVOTION

Rest, ceasing from striving and copious amounts of activity, is a weapon. We live in such a world of busyness. Busy seems to be the buzz word of our culture. How many times have you responded to a need in front of you with, "I am busy." How many times have you exclaimed, "I am so busy." What are we so busy doing?

Jesus, the Son of God, did not strive nor complain of being busy. He stated, "He did what He saw the Father doing." God created the world and then rested. I repeat God rested. We live in such a "Cram as much as you can into 24 hours," world. It does not leave time for God, rest, or even recuperation.

Every athlete knows the power of rest. If they overwork their bodies with no cycles of rest, it leads to gross fatigue and can result in injury. Our souls, spirits, and bodies need rest too. Part of rest is doing our part and trusting God to do the remainder.

Striving all the time is an indication of insecurity or lack of confidence in God. It says, "If I do not do this, it won't get done. God cannot be trusted to handle this." There are some things we are called to do, and others are outside our realm of responsibility. We can be so busy doing what is not our assignment that we are burned out and overworked for no reason.

Jesus frequently retreated from the crowds to be alone with the Father. He understood the power of intimacy with the Father and rest. There is refueling that happens when we stop doing and sink into being. One of my favorite quotes comes from missionary Heidi Baker. She stated, "Instead of being purpose driven, focus on being presence driven." What is God assigning to us for the day? What are we attaching to ourselves that is bringing about stress or strain or lack of rest?

It's okay to log off social media. It's okay to take a break. It's okay to take a vacation or staycation. It's okay to say no to another request for meeting up or ministry. It's okay to sneak away with God and just be in His presence.

In human relationships, it can grow annoying to try to connect with someone who is always busy, always glued to their smartphone, and never has time to just be with you. The invitation from God is, "Come away with me and be still. Be still and know I am God. Be still and know I can do more in a moment that you can achieve on your own in a lifetime."

We can also rest in the goodness of God. We can cease trying to figure everything out, trying to fix everything and everyone, and stop living out of a place of worry instead of peace. The invitation of God is rest.

REFLECTION

Have you been living in a place of rest and peace or busyness and worry?

What has driven you to forsake rest?

What promise has God given to those who set their minds on Him? (Hint: Isaiah 26:3)

PRAYER/DECLARATION

Papa God, I thank you for supernatural rest. I do not always need to be busy. I can rest just the way Jesus made rest a part of His lifestyle. Help me to be a person who lives in balance. I can relax, stop striving, and receive from you. Keep me from the buzz word of busy. I repent for forsaking the Sabbath rest and overloading my schedule. Help me to see what is a heavenly priority. I want to live a balanced and presence driven life. In Jesus mighty name, Amen.

I can rest and just be with God. Our intimacy grows in the moment of rest. I, like Jesus, can pull away just to be with the Father. I am refueled and replenished through purposeful times of rest. I enjoy resting with God. I do not need to worry; I can abide in the peace of God which surpasses all understanding.

DAY 29:

FREEDOM TO CREATE

*N*ow the Lord said to Moses," See, I have called by name Bezalel, son of Uri, the son of Hur, of the tribe of Judah. I have filled him with the Spirit of God in wisdom and skill, in understanding and intelligence, in knowledge, and in all kinds of craftsmanship, to make artistic designs for work in gold, in silver, and in bronze, and in the cutting of stones for settings, and in the carving of wood, to work in all kinds of craftsmanship.

And behold, I Myself have appointed with him Oholiab, son of Ahisamach, of the tribe of Dan; to all who are wise-hearted I have given the skill and ability to make everything that I have commanded you: the Tent of Meeting, the ark of the Testimony, the mercy seat that is upon it, all the furnishings of the tent— the table [for the bread] and its utensils, the pure gold lampstand with all its utensils, the [golden] altar of incense, the [bronze] altar of burnt offering with all its utensils, the basin and its base—the finely worked garments, the holy garments for Aaron the [high] priest and the garments for his sons to minister *as priests, and the anointing oil and the sweet and fragrant incense for the Holy Place. They are to make them according to all that I have commanded you." (Exodus 31:1-11 AMP).*

DEVOTION

God, the Creator of the Universe, has given creative gifts to His children. If we are in Christ (placed our faith in Jesus and follow Him), the Spirit of God abides with us. God loves creating. God is creative. Everything on earth points to the majesty and creativity of God. If we look around at the diversity of plant life, animal life, and even human life, all we see is creativity in motion. The mind of God is unlimited.

God invites us by His Spirit to create. Bezalel was infused with the Spirit of God in wisdom and skill, understanding and intelligence, in knowledge, and all kinds of craftsmanship. God's Spirit enabled him to create. God partnered with human beings to create and craft the Tent of Meeting, the ark of the Testimony, the mercy seat, and the furnishings for the tent.

The Spirit of the Creator lives in every born-again believer. You may be thinking, "There is not a creative bone in my body." If the Spirit of God lives in you, creativity lives in you. Maybe your creativity does not manifest in painting, singing, songwriting, sculpting, design, architecture, or engineering. It may manifest in witty ideas of how to do things, connect people, teach something, or another way. My encouragement is think of yourself as someone designed for creativity.

If we can believe God for wisdom, we can believe God for creativity, bright ideas, inventions, and innovations. God loves to share not only knowledge and understanding, He longs to share gifts and talents as well. We can see this in the lives of many in the Bible. God gave them wisdom, insight, skill, expertise, understanding, and creative ideas.

God invites us to move beyond our perceptions of who we are to see what He sees when He looks at us. He encourages a more in-depth exploration of who He is, and in knowing the Creator, we find our creative outlets.

I love music, yet never thought of myself as a songwriter until I went to a songwriting class. I would have told you before that I did not write music, yet the leader of that class said to us that we could all write music. So, I sat down with my guitar and began to write. I have written over a dozen songs.

It is imperative we take the lid off who we think we are and grow into godly confidence. We can do more than we can imagine with Jesus. The most creative Being in the Universe says, "Come create with Me."

REFLECTION

Do you see yourself as creative?

Have you had an idea that just popped up in your mind and spirit that seemed to have creative flow?

After today's devotion, do you think you can step out and create with God?

PRAYER/DECLARATION

Papa God, thank you for the creative Holy Spirit. Thank you for creativity. Help me to hear from you and listen to witty innovations, ideas, and innovative solutions. Show me the creativity you placed in my spirit and soul. Awaken the creativity within me. Show me where to invest creative talents that will bring you great glory.

God created me in His image. In Christ, the Creative One lives in me. I can create with God. God gives us skill, wisdom, understanding, and access to His creativity. I will be open to creating with God and listening to His ideas, innovations, and problem-solving skills. I lend my ear to hear from God.

DAY 30:

FREEDOM TO DREAM

D*elight yourself in the Lord, and He will give you the desires and petitions of your heart. (Psalm 37:4 AMP).*

For everyone who keeps on asking [persistently], receives; and he who keeps on seeking [persistently], finds; and to him who keeps on knocking [persistently], the door will be opened. What father among you, if his son asks for a fish, will give him a snake instead of a fish? Or if he asks for an egg, will give him a scorpion? (Luke 11:10-12 AMP).

DEVOTION

Awaken the dreamers, the ones who move beyond the mundane and are bold to explore unknown territory with God. Dreamers are the visionaries. They believe beyond what they see in the natural to what could be. Dreamers see possibilities and not just realities. Dreamers believe that when their ideas with God are spoken out, there will be an eventual manifestation of that dream.

I love that children dream. They mostly do not dream of being mediocre, a failure, a nobody, or insignificant. Children dream with confidence of being heroes, world changers, and children have fun imagining the endless possibilities.

There is something that happens to adults to silence the dreams. It becomes about surviving, instead of thriving. It becomes about earning paychecks, and not building a desirable legacy. The hopes of changing the world are replaced with, "I will settle for not having a super challenge this week." The dreamer is lulled to sleep, and the eagerness to dream diminishes.

Sometimes the confidence to dream is quenched by past disappointments and rejections. You may have stepped out in the past only to have your vision shot down by someone. Maybe you tried, and it seemed like an utter failure. Perhaps you have given your all, and the return was minimal. You hung up the dreamer's cape and threw out the dreaming. Maybe you have never dreamed with God. Know that His dreams with you and for you are exceedingly, abundantly, above all you could ask or imagine (Ephesians 3:20).

I want to encourage you to delight yourself in the Lord and dream again. Maybe you are thinking, "I do not have a dream. I have not dreamed in forever, I do not even know where to start," and that's okay. Luke 11:10-12 invites us to ask of God, to seek God, and know that what we ask of God according to His will (it's not sinful, immoral, or harmful) will be given to us. God loves to see His children dream. A good parent wants the very best for their child and dreaming with God requires faith (God will do what He said) and builds confidence (look at all my dreams fulfilled with God).

When we know God and know how much God loves us, we can trust that we can safely dream with God. We can believe that God will not let us down. God does not desire to let us down. God also does not want us just to survive life. God wants us to thrive. To thrive means to prosper, and flourish. God does not wish to diminish our dreams nor quench our childlike dreaming. He desires to purify our desires, dreams, and exceed them!

REFLECTION

What were some of your childhood dreams? Have you pursued any of those dreams?

Do you see yourself as just surviving or thriving?

If you are just surviving, what has gotten in the way of your dreaming with God?

Bonus Activity: Grab a pen and paper and write out some dreams with God. At the top of the page, write "Dreams with God." Then make three columns. One that says, "I can do this easily," another that says "Requires divine help," and the last column "Seems impossible." I want you to date this page and pray over it with God. The purpose of this activity is to get the dream out of the head and heart and onto paper. Write the vision. I want you to complete this activity with the thought that there are no limits on what can be done.

PRAYER/DECLARATION

Papa God, thank you for dreaming with me and inviting me into the world of dreams. I want to think outside the box and believe for unlimited possibilities. I ask for your help to imagine impossibilities made possible and to hope again. Heal wounds on my soul from the past by the power of Jesus. I desire to expect the very best from you. I want my legacy to be one of fulfilled God dreams. Give me the courage to take risks and see the fulfillment of Ephesians 3:20 dreams.

God desires for me to dream with Him. Part of my intimacy with God is growing in confidence that God wants my dreams with Him to come true. God loves me and cares about the desires of my heart. God loves to see me dream. There are dreams within me waiting to be released. I am a dreamer. I believe I will see the manifestation of many dreams with God.

BONUS POEM:
DO YOU KNOW WHO YOU ARE?

Excerpt from I Thought I Knew What Love Was
Written by Erin Lamb © 2011
May 12, 2008

Do you know who you are.

Do you know who you really, truly are,

without the name of your natural father,

or the labels given to you by man?

For I have given you My name,

and I call you, "Chosen."

If you knew who you were;

the integrity of the kernels of faith

and spiritual gifts I have placed inside you;

you would no longer bow your head in shame.

You would understand that for all your sins I stood in your place.

Do you know who you are?

You are not defined by your past,

or even your present.

Each day is just setting the stage to tell your story;

where you are,

is not where you are going.

I do not define you by what you have done,

what you are doing,

or what you will do.

I have placed My name on you.

Your body is My temple,

and I long to always reside with you.

When you sleep and rest in the night hours,

I am awake.

I am watching over you,

waiting enthusiastically until you awaken.

I am longing to meet with you

and shower you with My love.

My love is constant, steadfast, and as enduring as the sun.

Do you know who you are?

I have set you apart to be holy;

for I am Holy.

You are clothed in My righteousness.

You cannot earn My redemption.

It is freely given by your faith and obedience.

My love for you is not dependent upon what you do,

or what you fail to do.

What I accomplished on the cross is finished.

The veil was torn

and your access granted to the most sacred of all.

When you confess your sins

and forgive others,

you are forgiven.

DO YOU KNOW WHO YOU ARE?

Your slate is wiped completely clean.

My blood covers each and every sin,

so you no longer have to feel guilt or shame.

Do you know who you are?

If only you could see,

what I see.

I wish you could view yourself through My eyes,

the eyes of love.

I have embraced you in the darkness of the night,

knowing that I wanted you.

My heart's desire was, and is, to search for you,

to look for you,

to pursue you;

what I have for you is beyond your wildest imaginings.

I long to give you more of Me.

I know that My love can satisfy even your most profound needs.

I created you,

looked upon you,

and smiled on who I had made.

I am shaping and molding you into the person I created you to be.

I want the world to get a glimpse of My glory.

I long to radiate from you,

for all the world to see

My glorious splendor.

I am the One who created everything.

There is not one who can rank above Me.

I am above all,

in all, and I have the power to change, create, and breathe life into any

dead thing.

Your right now is simply an infinitesimal step along the journey which leads you closer to Me.

No matter what label the world chooses to place on you, the only significant one

is the one I have given,

and I have called you, My child.

I call you My friend, My co-laborer,

My dearly loved one, My family, and most of all, I call you redeemed.

Do you know who you are?

If only you could see what I see,

for you were birthed with a purpose; a story uniquely written for you.

I have the ability to turn even the fine particles of the earth into

something that is living and breathing.

Won't you surrender your identity to Me?

Trust that I am the One who will make you complete.

You are not to be compared to any other human being. I made you to be you,

and I have placed on you My fingerprints.

I placed together your DNA, and there is no one exactly like you. You are My masterpiece.

Don't look to this world to define you; look to Me.

I am the One who designed you. I know everything about you.

I know every breath you take, and your life is not in vain.

Into you I breathed life,

so I might use you

to reflect My image.

You are My image bearer.

Do you know who you are?

Do you understand the authority you have been given, in My name?

You were created to be about My business.

You were created to reach out to the least, the last, and the lost. You

were created to worship the Creator
and not created things.
Your life is not your own;
it was purchased with My blood.
I took your lashes.
I carried your infirmities.
I took the nails for you.
I took your shame.
You no longer stand condemned,
but freely can receive My grace.
Do you know who you are?
Chosen one,
you are set apart to bear the image of the King.
You are My child.
You are the one I love.
You are the one I adore,
and I know you personally.
Each breath you take is sweet music to My ears.
It is the sound of the breath I Myself have placed there.
I know you.
I made you for a reason.
Each gift, placed inside you, is to play an integral part
in reflecting My kingdom,
in reflecting My creativity, and My love.
You are not a mistake,
a mishap,
or a blip on the screen of life.
You are not insignificant;
I knew you before the foundations of the earth.
Before your parents knew you,

I called you by name
and said, "This one belongs to Me."
I know your name,
and I will always know your name.
I cannot forget you.
I know the measure of your days;
I have them numbered, and your time is written on My hands. Your end
will be better than the beginning, if you will trust Me,
even with the things you don't understand. I am the God of all creation.
If you cannot answer who you are,
look to Me.
Do you know who I am?
I have created you in My image,
and I delight in all that I have made.
I do not make mistakes.
I love you, now,
and I will love you, always.

CONCLUSION

God loves His children more than an earthly parent loves their children. The heart of God is to see His children confident and free. Godly confidence is not arrogance, nor is it self-depreciation. It is a proper assessment of oneself relating to God. We are of the God kind. It does not mean we are demigods, nor are we to be worshipped. It does say that we come from a royal family, and God does not create junk.

Jesus paid such a high price to free us. This freedom is not just saving freedom, so we are not lost in eternal damnation. It is a freedom to thrive, even in the most challenging situations. Jesus paid to free not only our spirit; He paid to free our souls.

My prayer is that this devotional has drawn you closer to the heart of God and provided insight into what Jesus paid for on that rugged cross.

My prayers will continue to be that you flourish, shine, and fulfill the fullness of God's prophetic purposes for your life. You were created to thrive and prosper. You are a handcrafted, designer original.

God believes in you. I believe in you too! I decree and declare to you:

You are confident and free.

You have a remarkable destiny.

You are handcrafted by God.

You bear the mark of royalty.

You were born for such a time as this.

You are not limited if you are rooted in God.

The possibilities are beyond what you can imagine with God.

The best is yet to come.

Your destiny will bring God great glory.

ABOUT THE AUTHOR

Erin Lamb is an Engineer and Research Scientist. She is also involved in city outreach, street ministry, street evangelism and local/overseas missions. She founded two ministry initiatives: Operation God is Love (OGL) and Ignite Fellowship. OGL is a city initiative to the poor, least, last, and lost. Ignite Fellowship is a women's discipleship group, bible study, and involves prophetic intercession. Ms. Lamb also enjoys leading worship, creating art, music, and writing poetry.

Published Books:

I Thought I Knew What Love Was; The Journey to Intimacy with God.

Book Website: www.IthoughtIknewwhatlovewas.com

Ministry Website: www.OperationGodisLove.org

Business Website: https://www.empowered-free.com

Made in the USA
Middletown, DE
17 June 2023

32790130R00080